MINIMALISTIC COLORING BOOK

Copyright © 2024 OnTrend Publishing
All rights reserved.

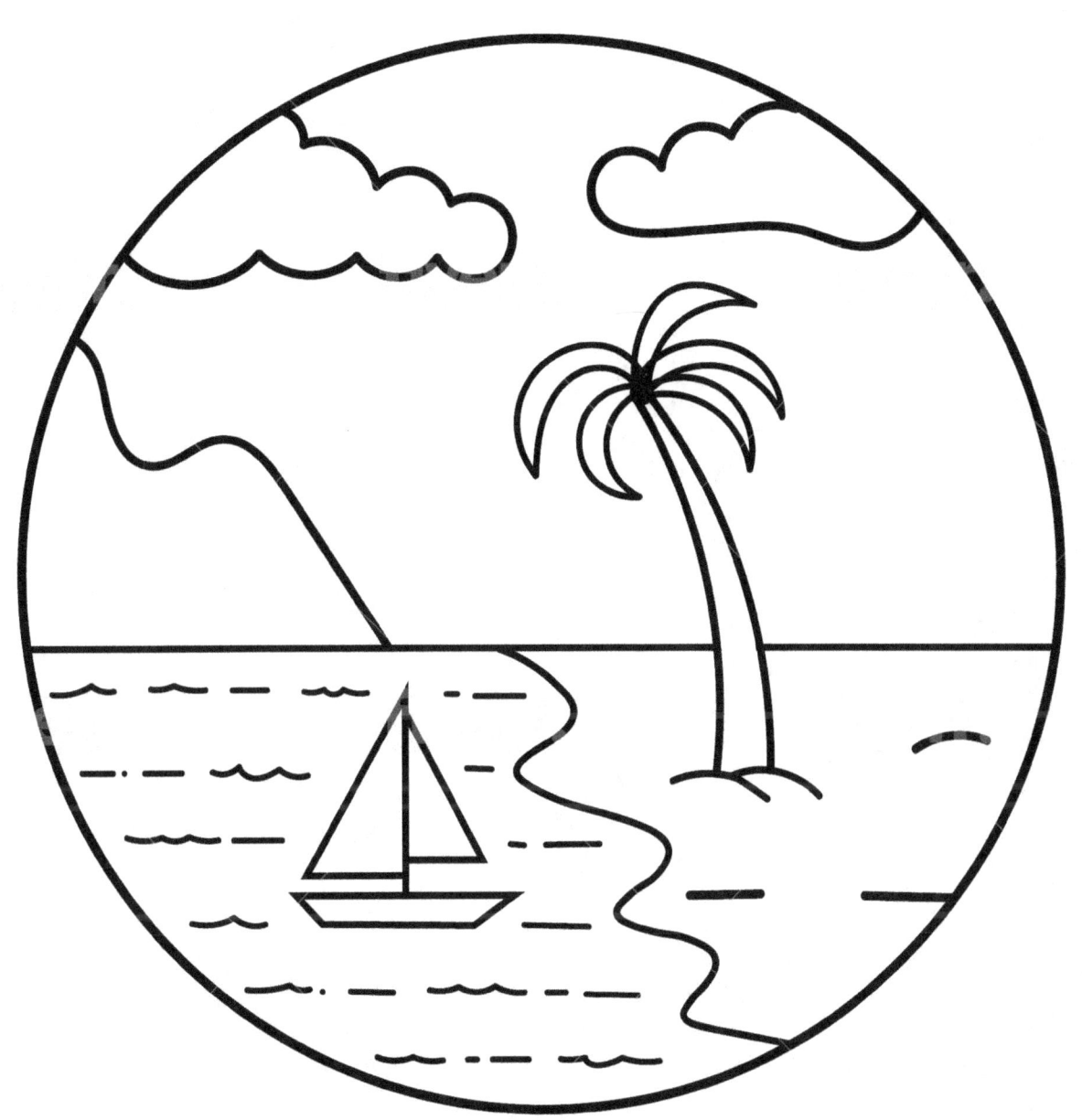

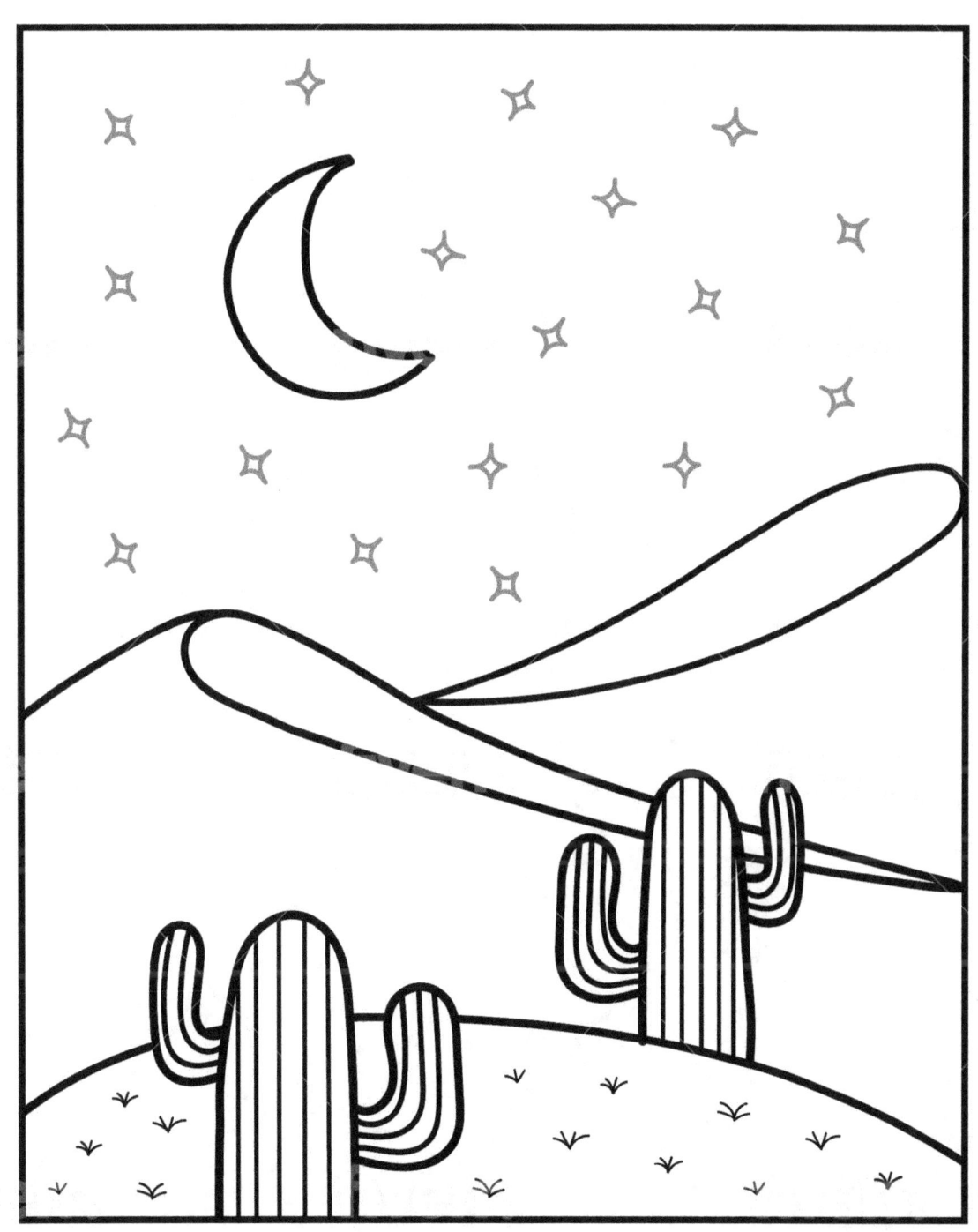

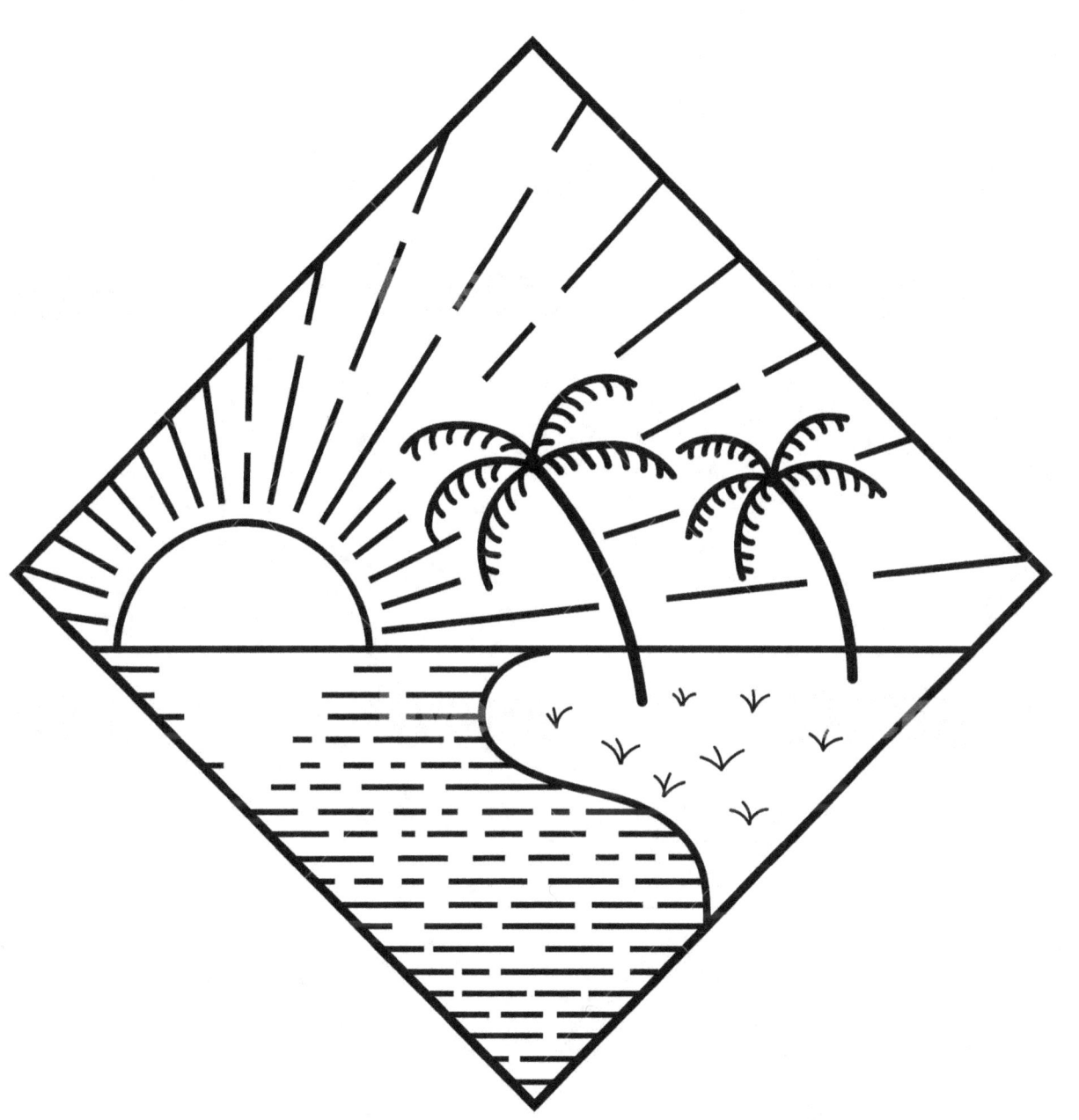

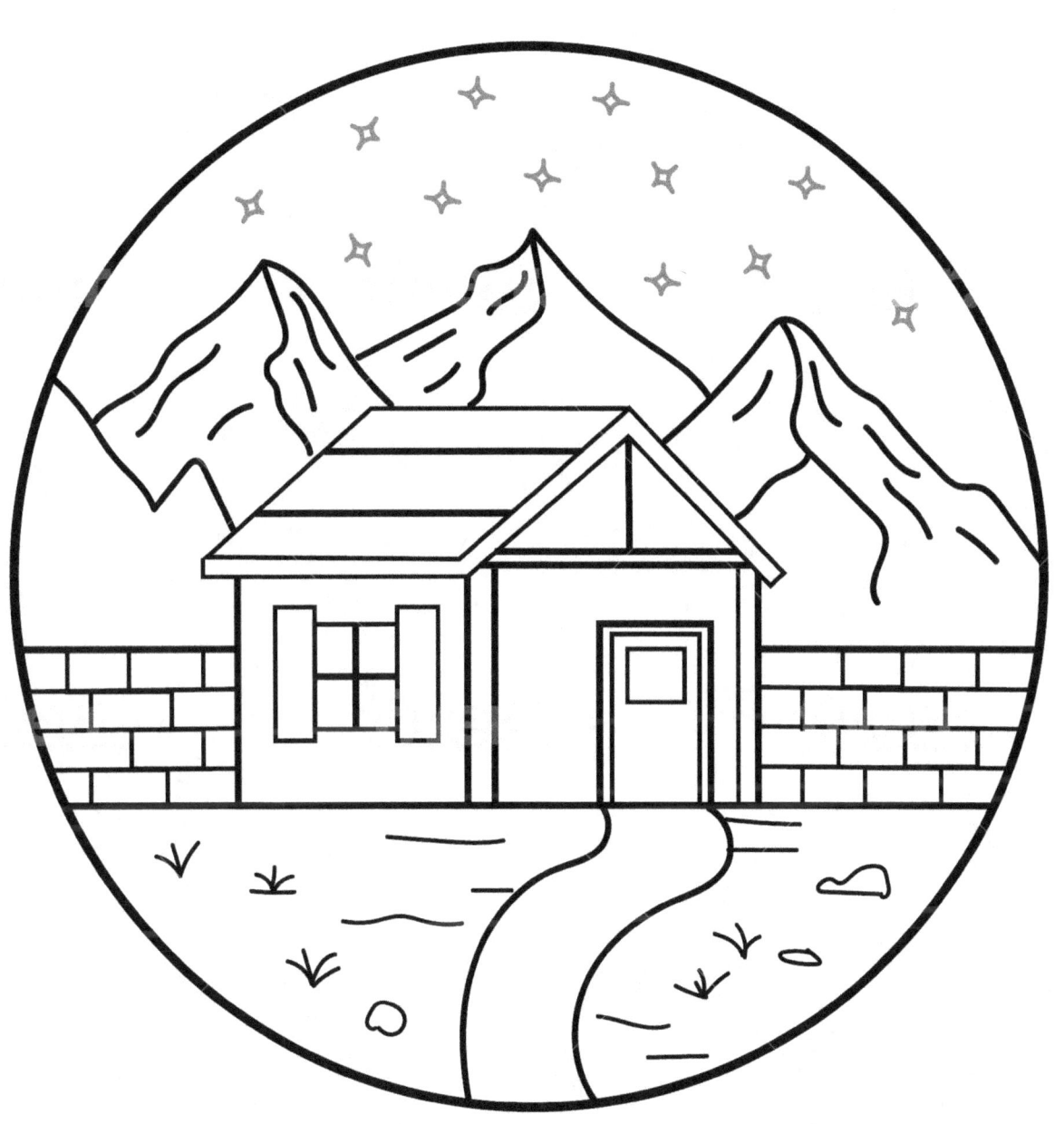

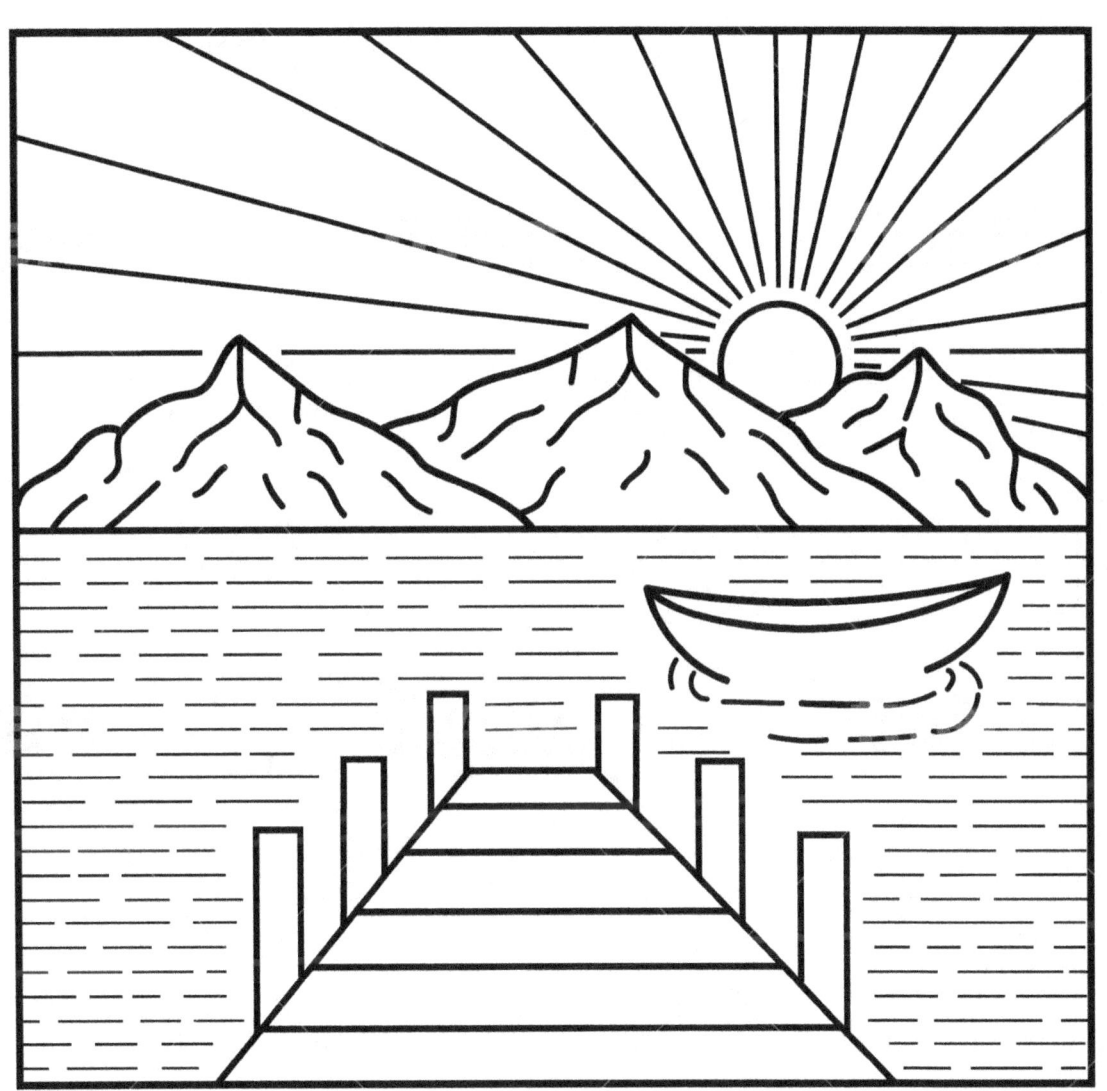

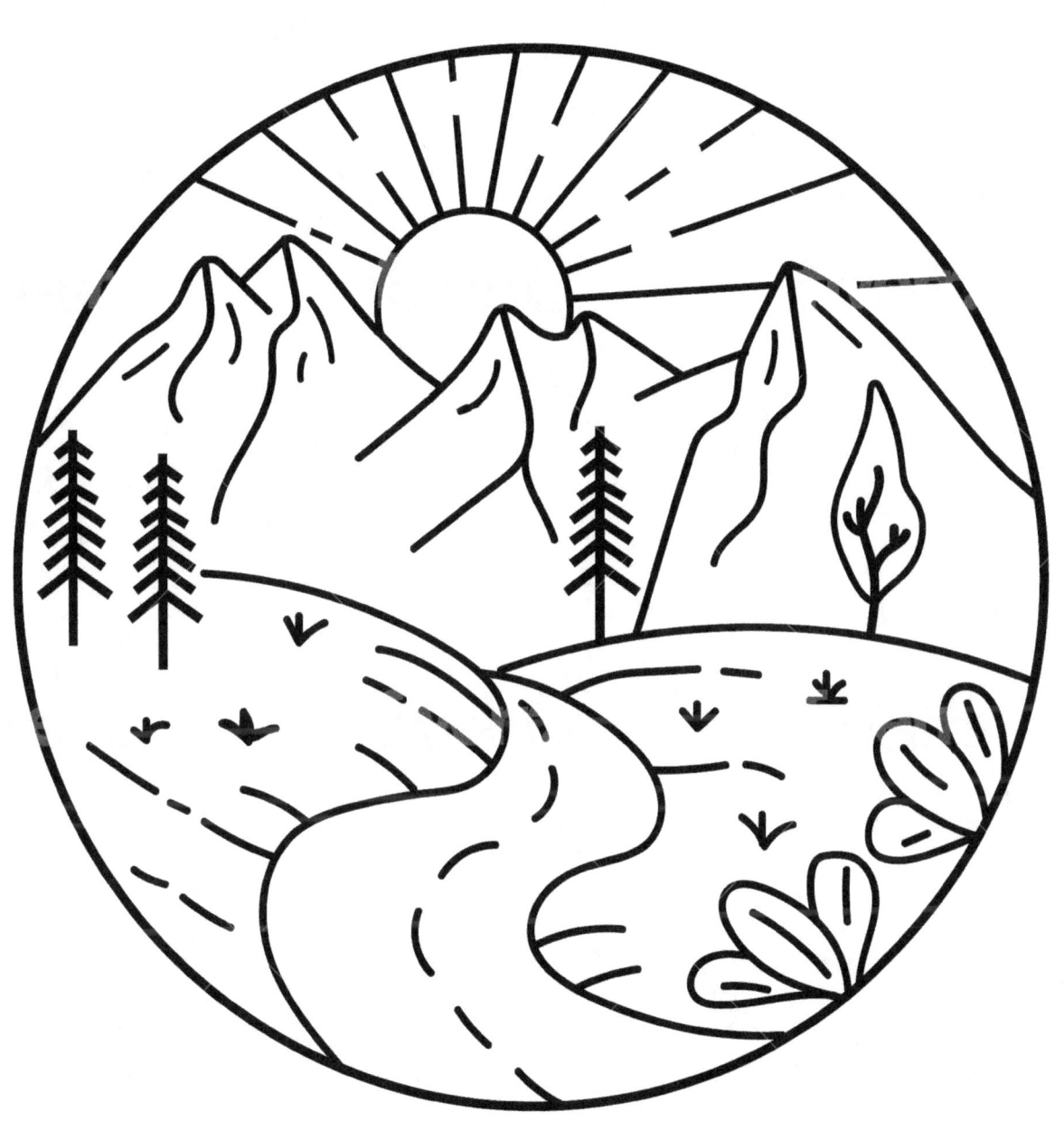

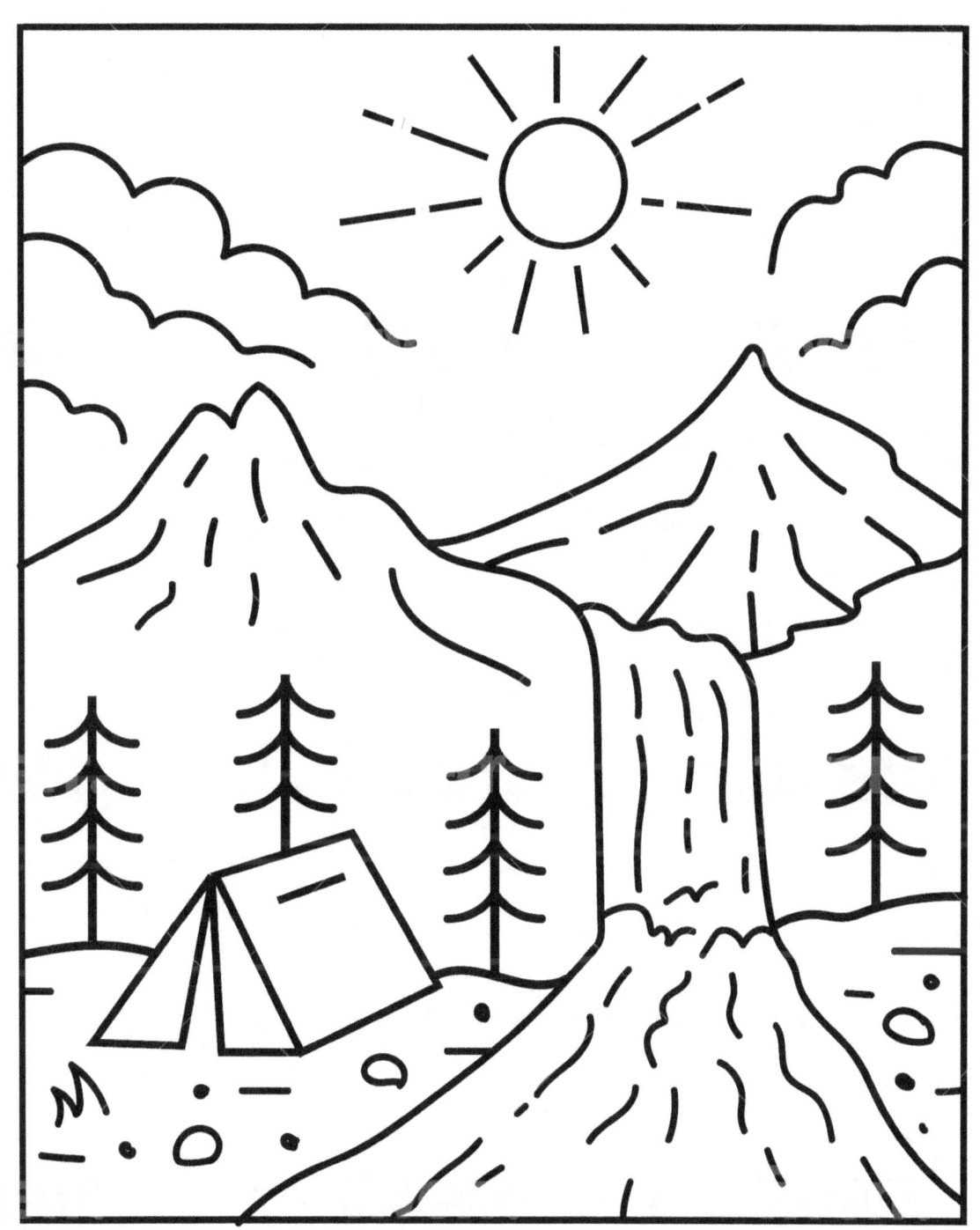

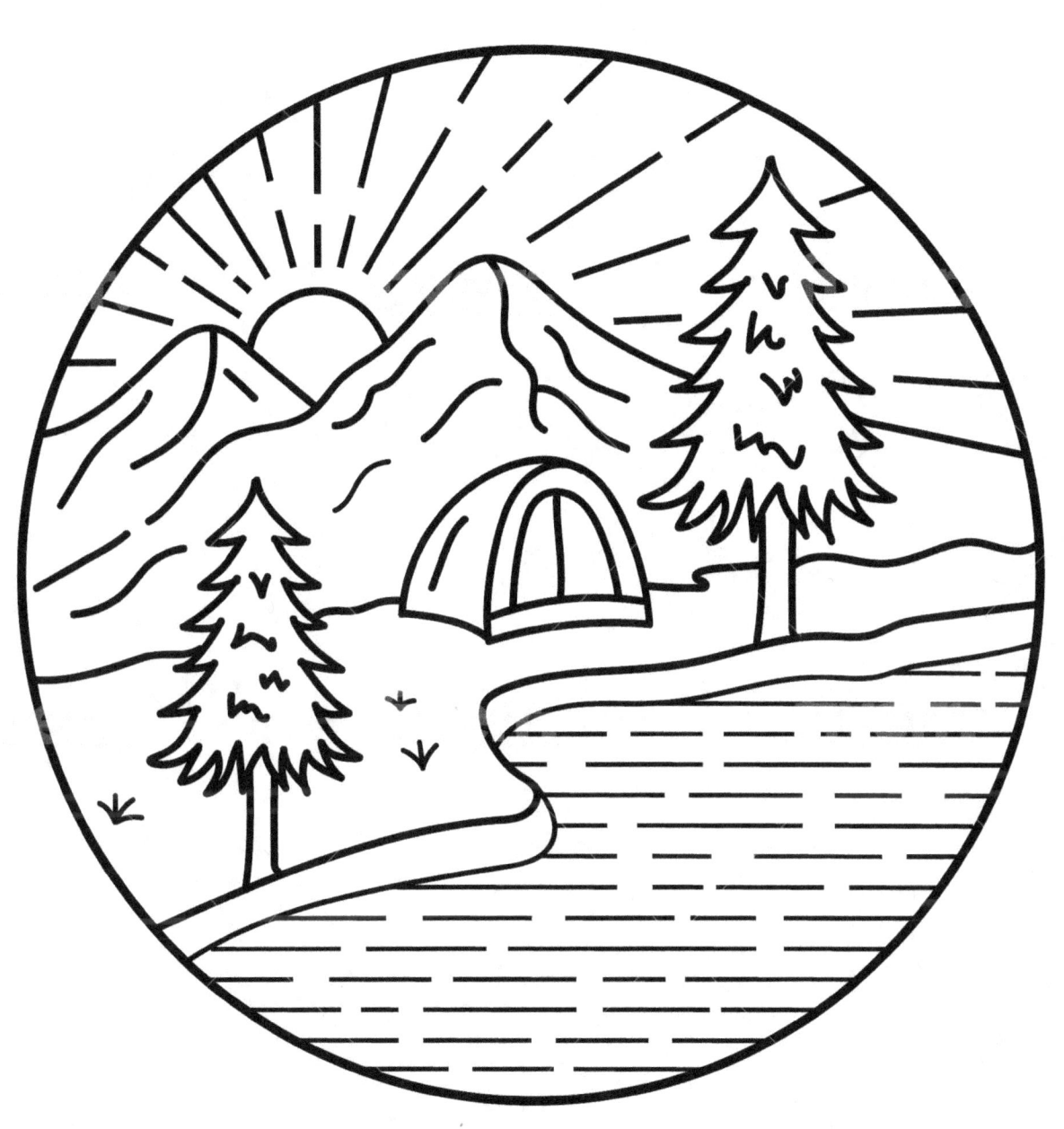

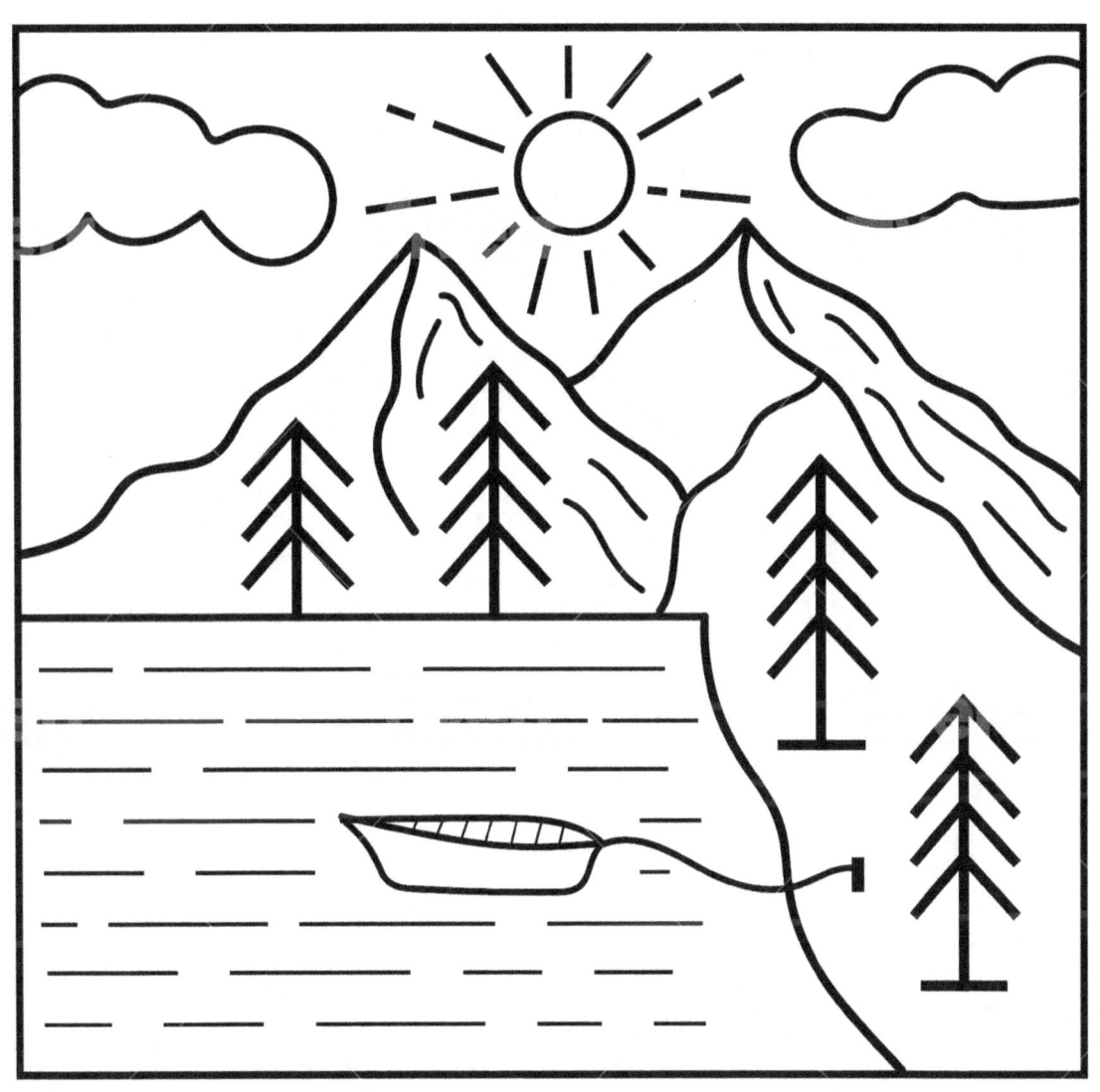

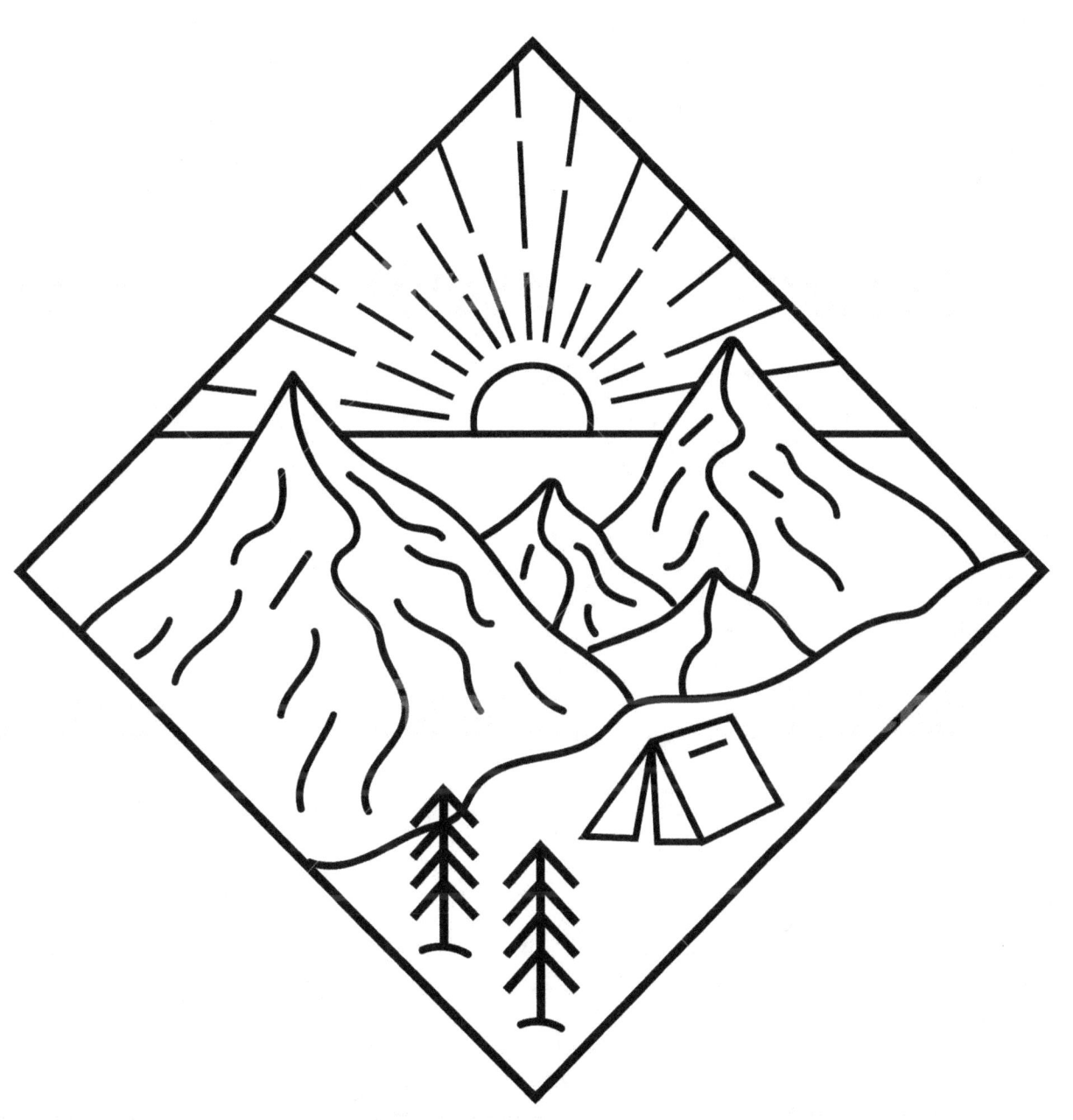

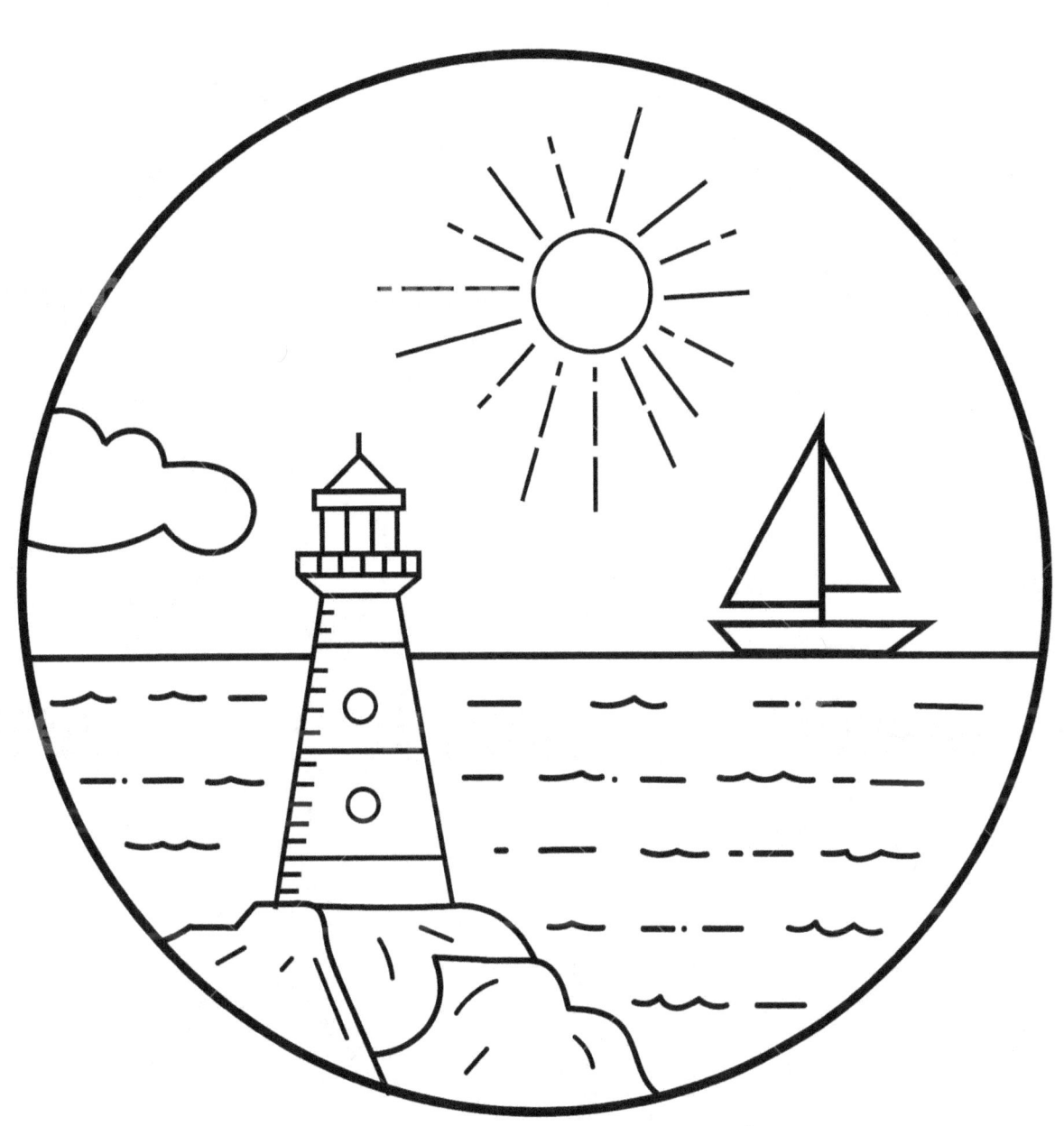

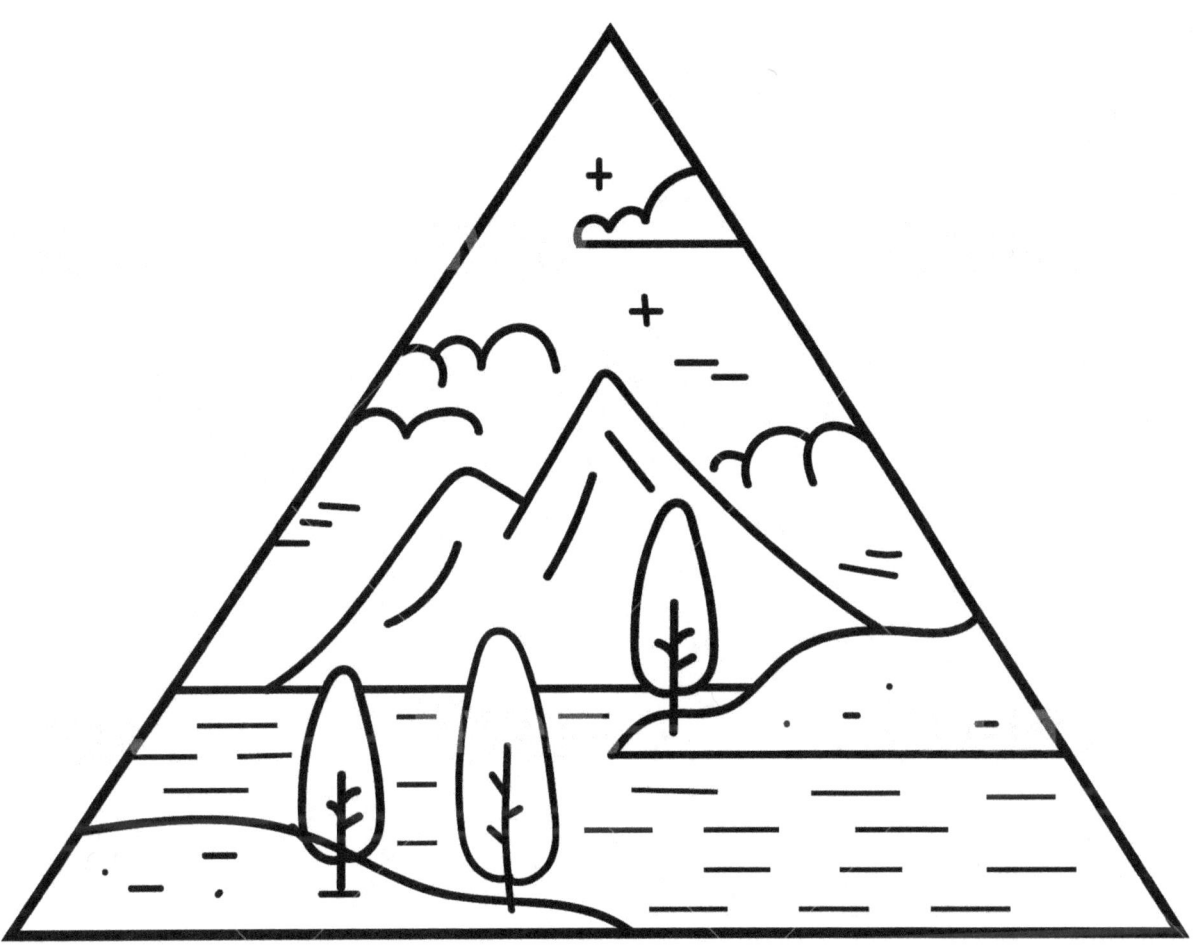

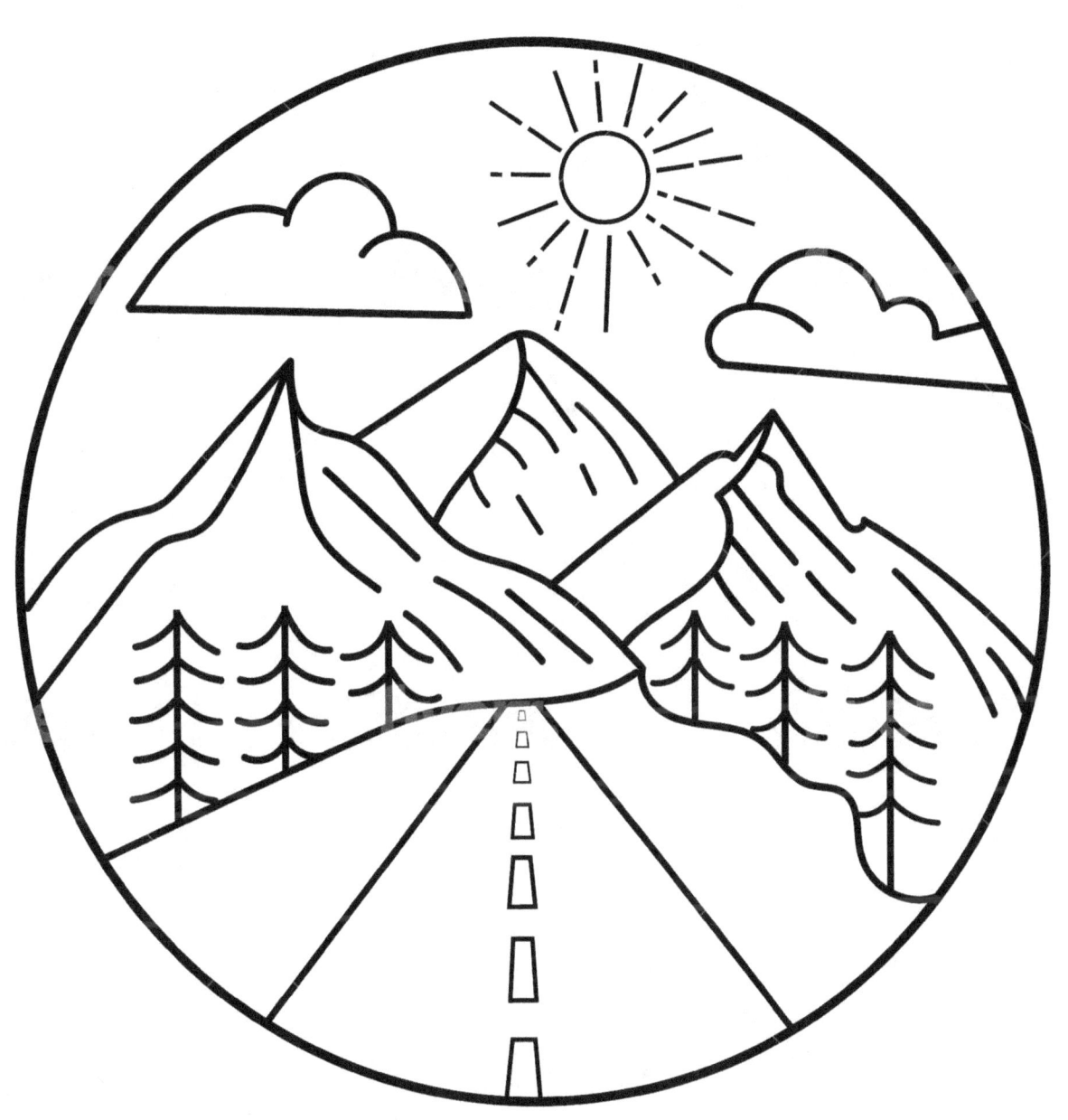

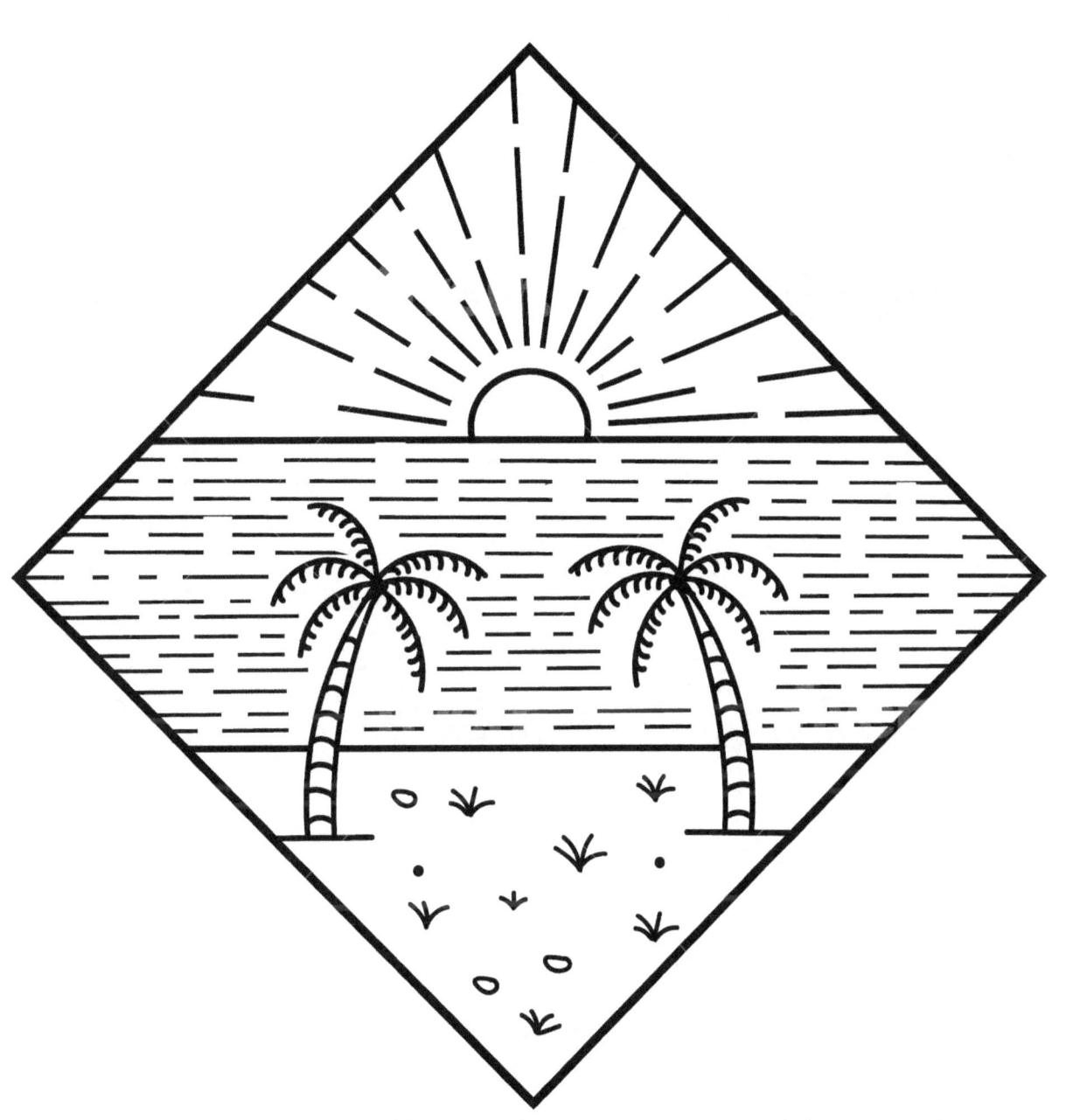

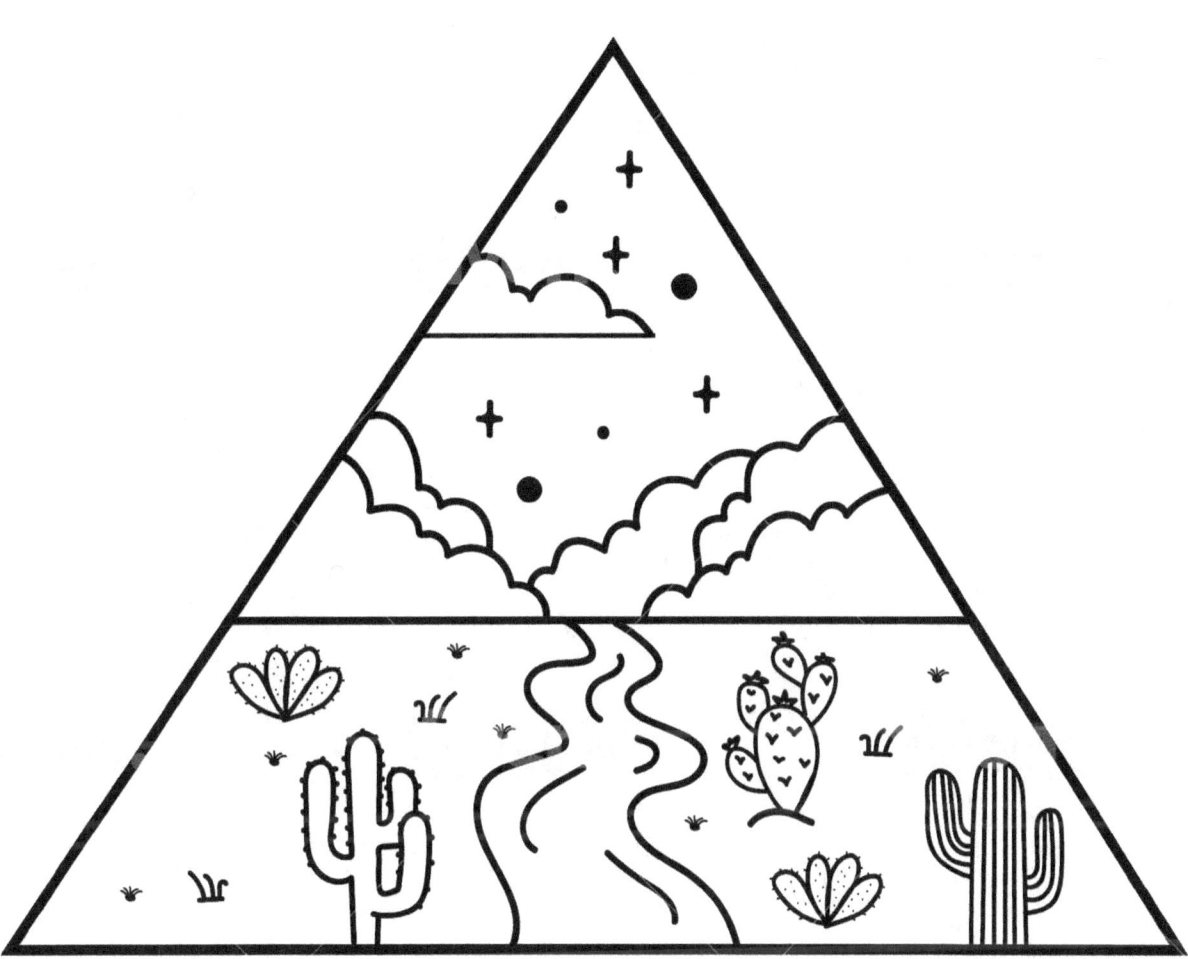

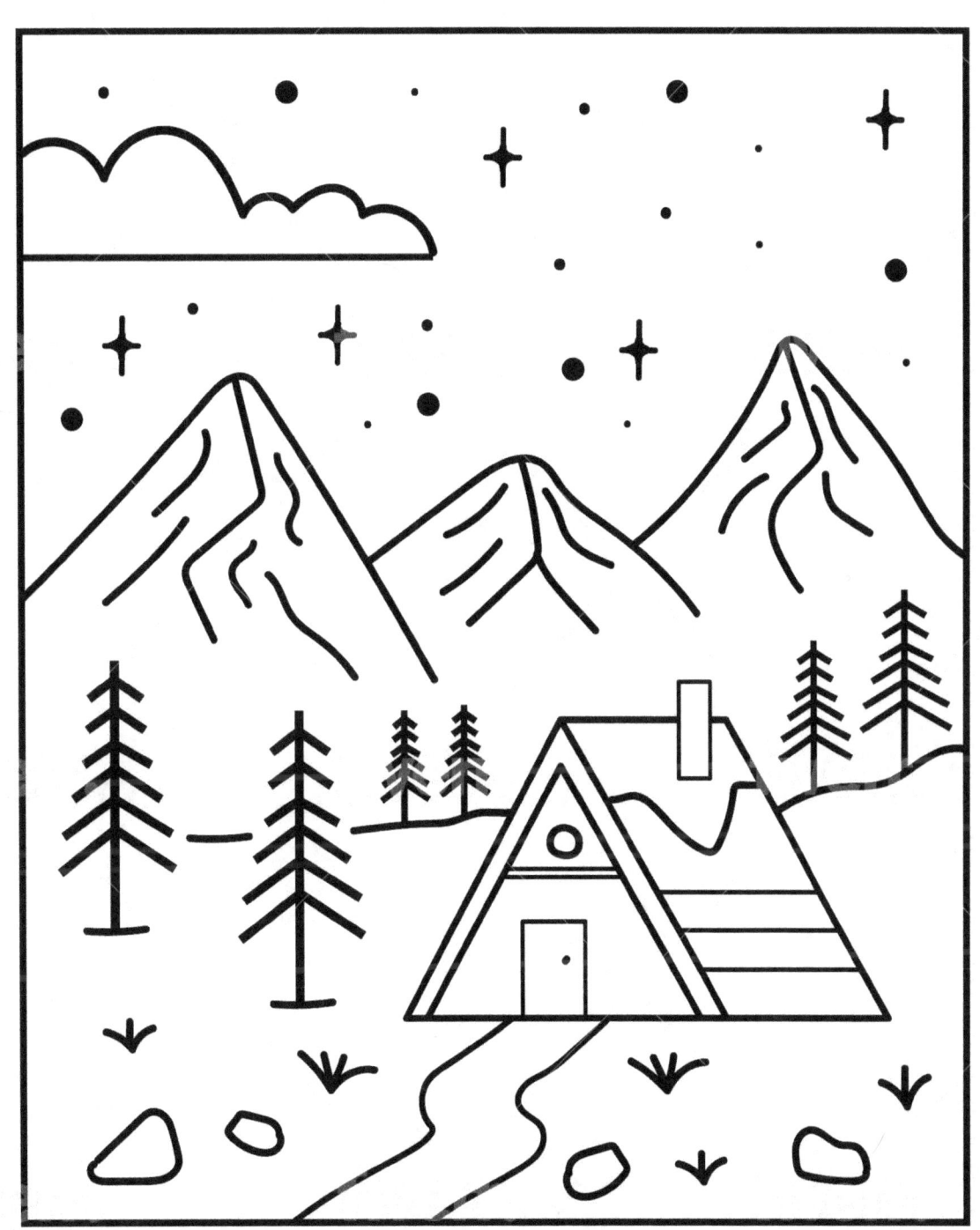

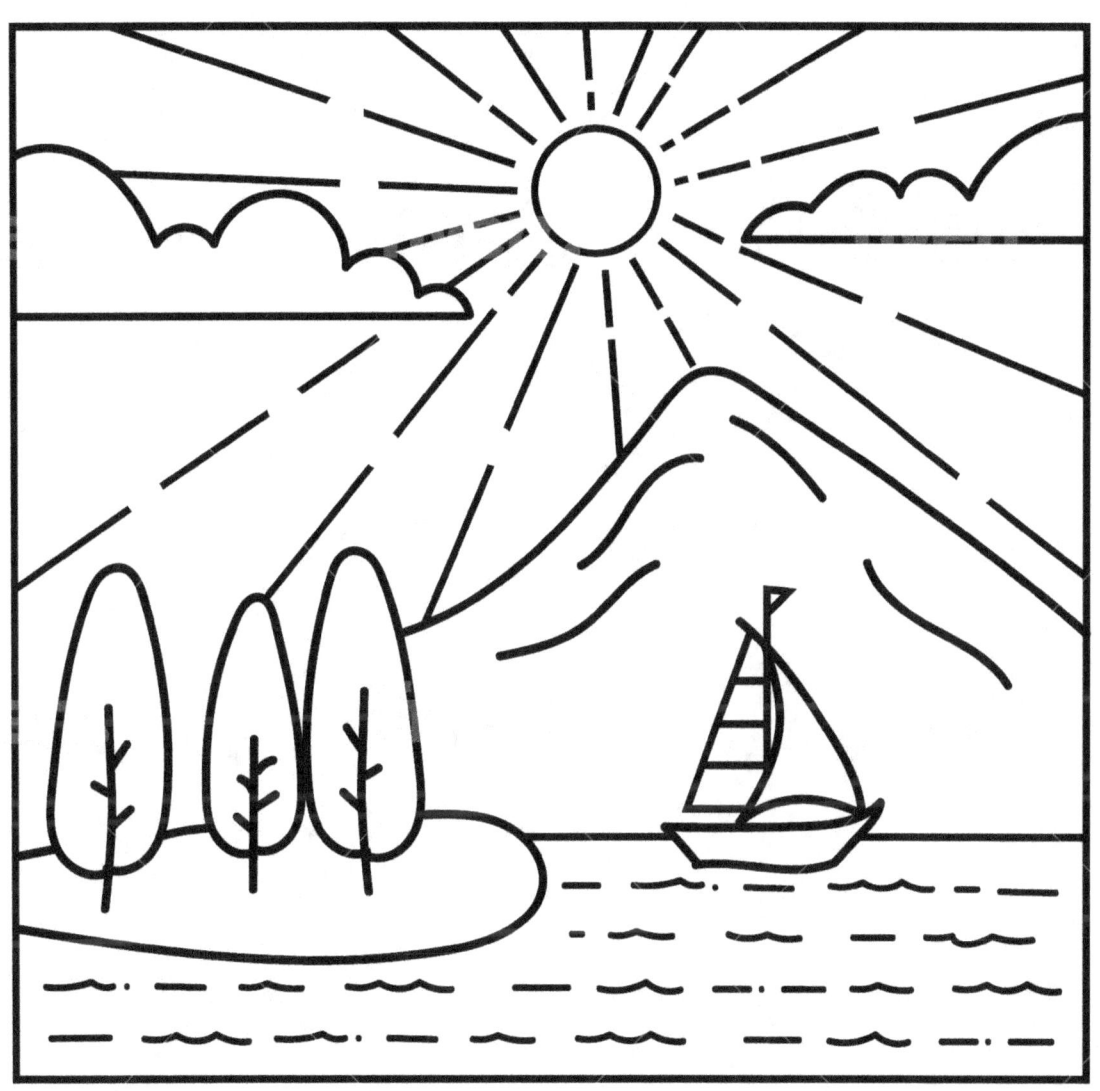

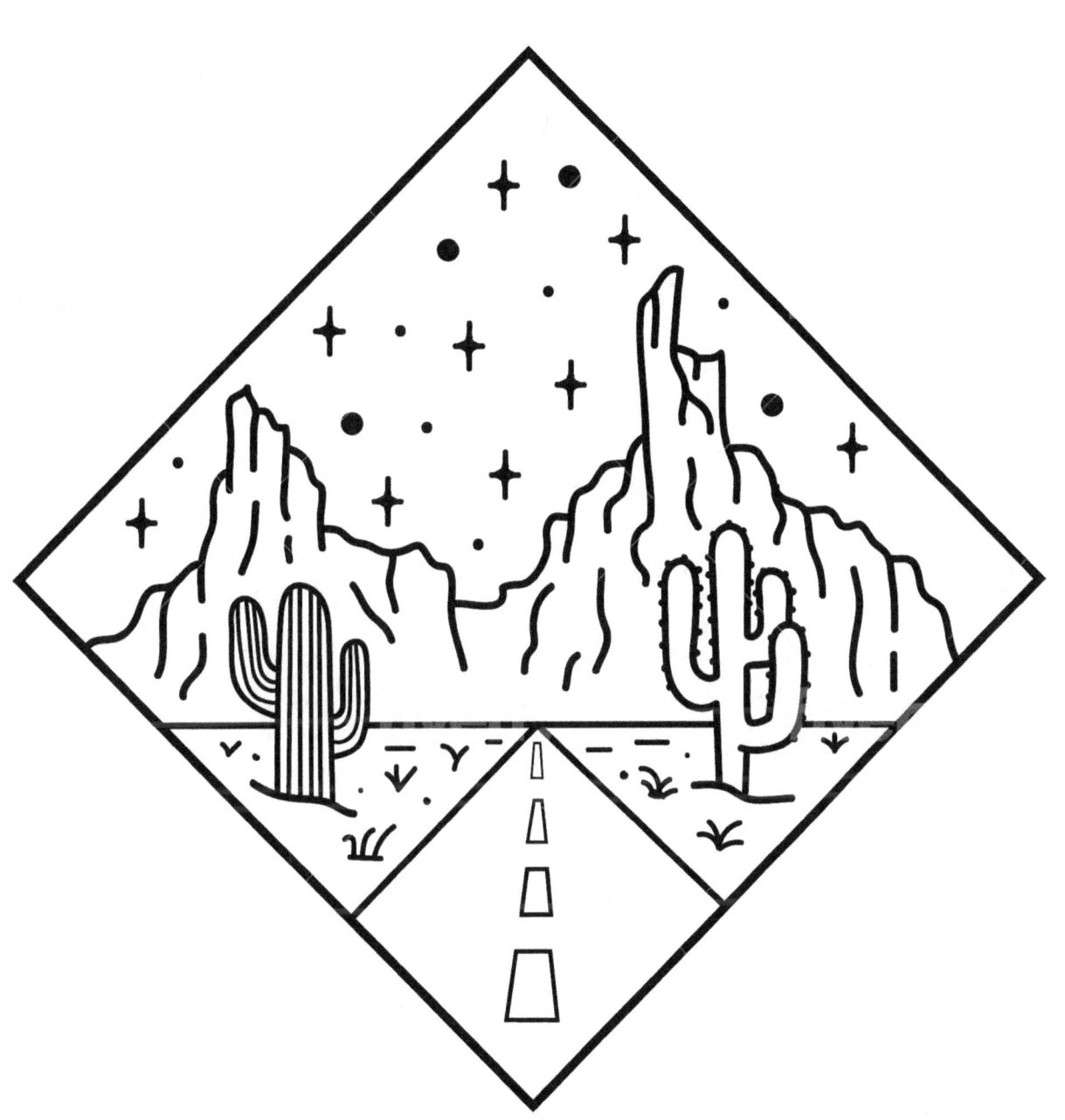

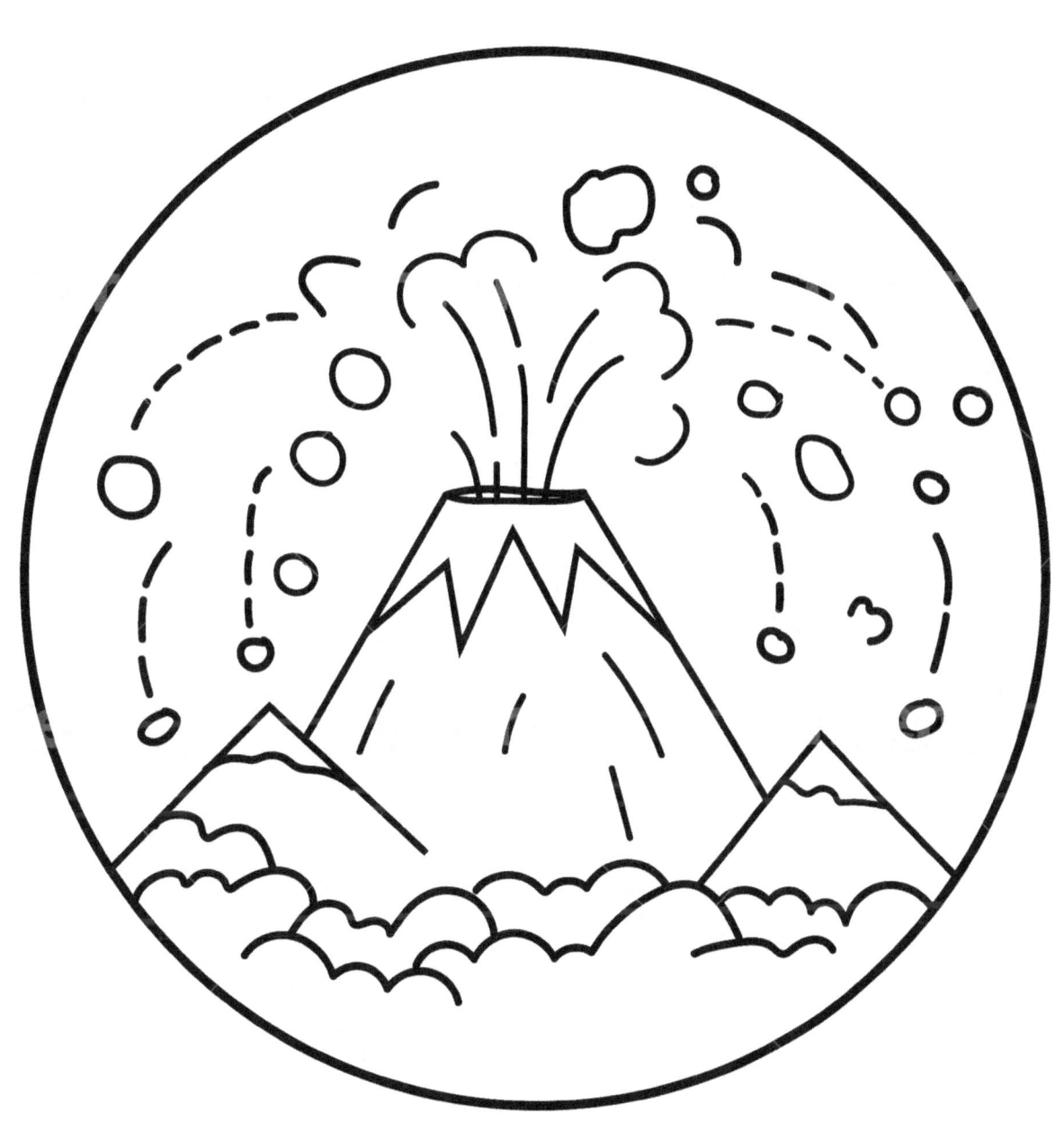

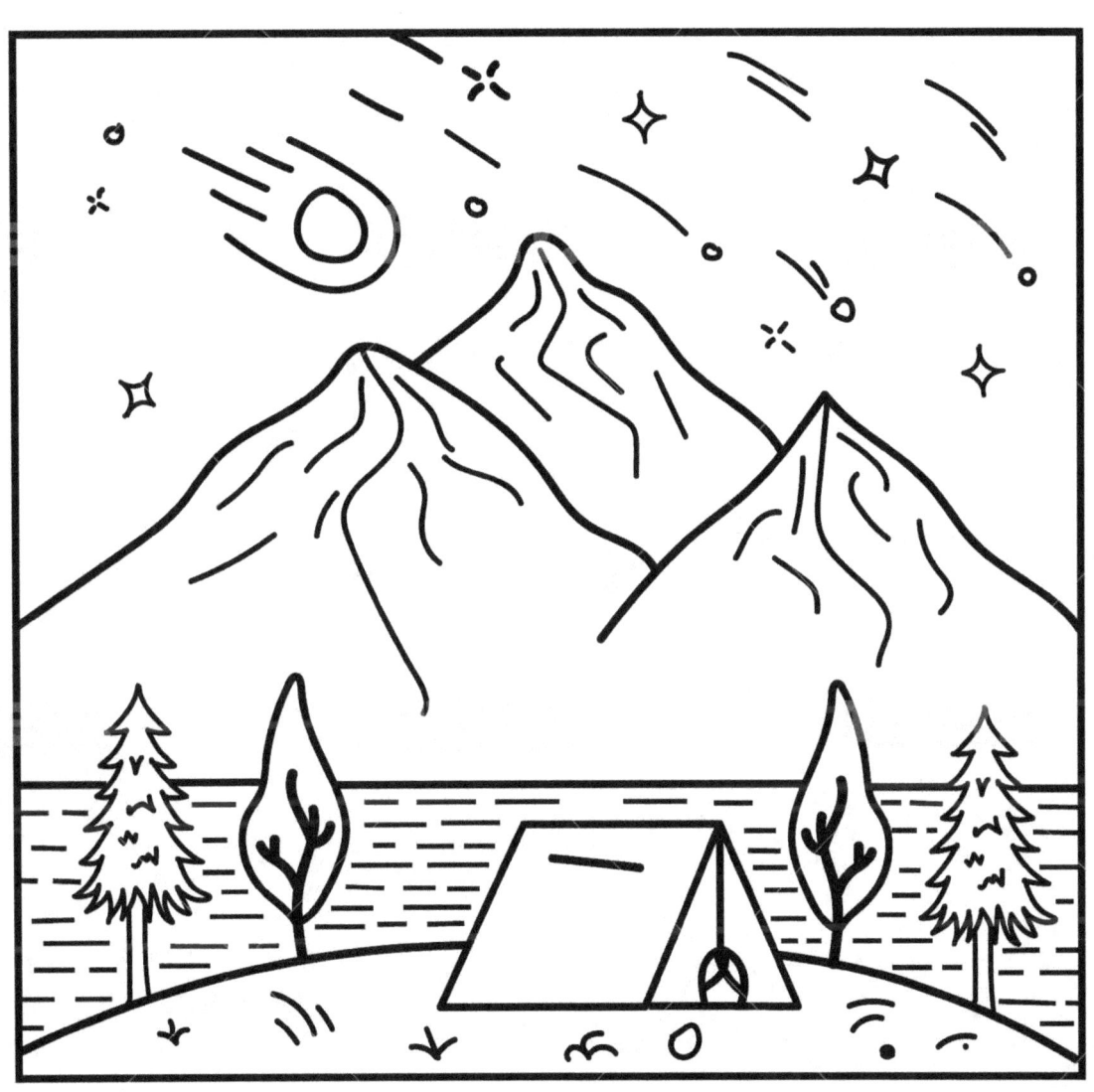

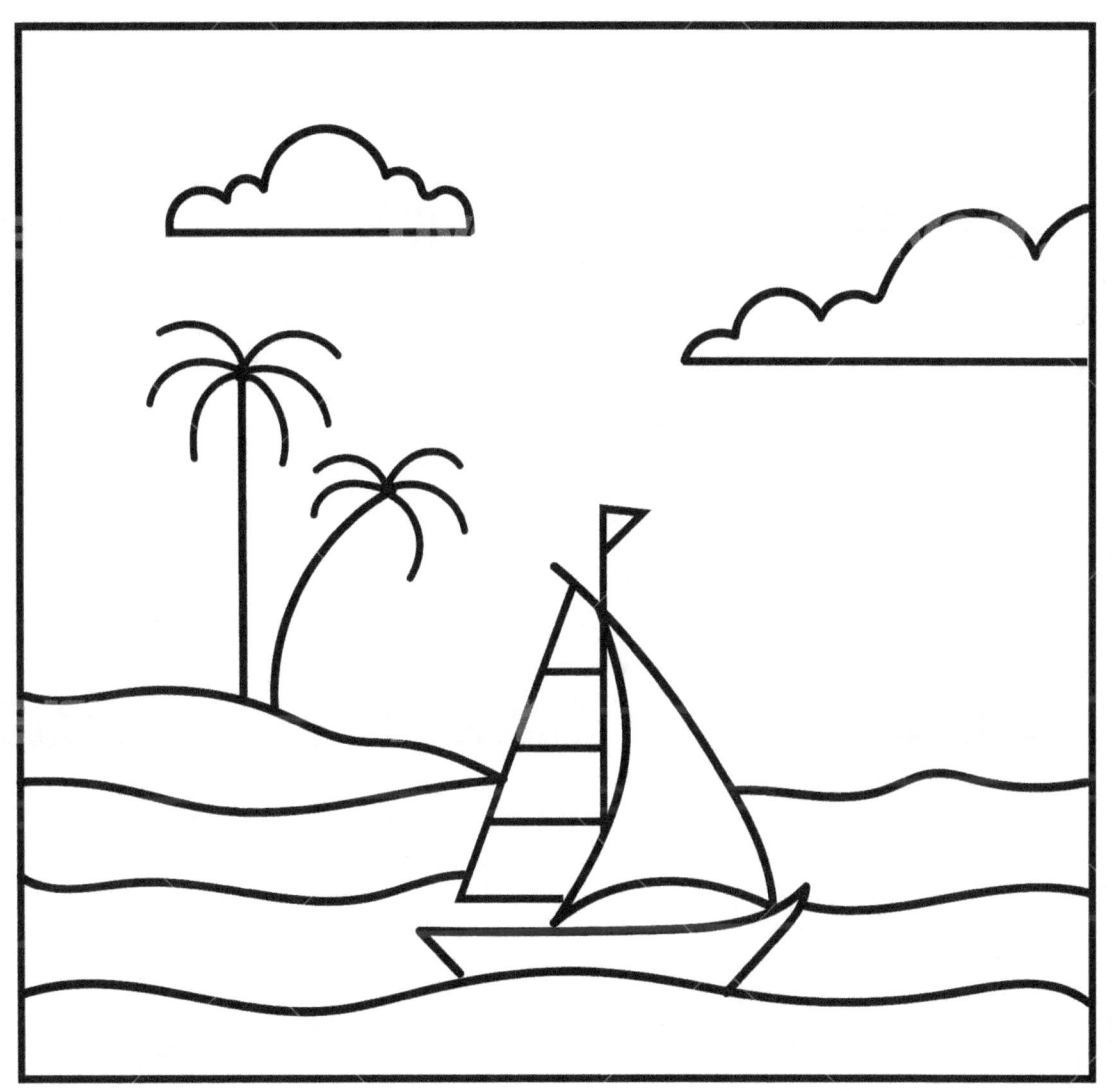

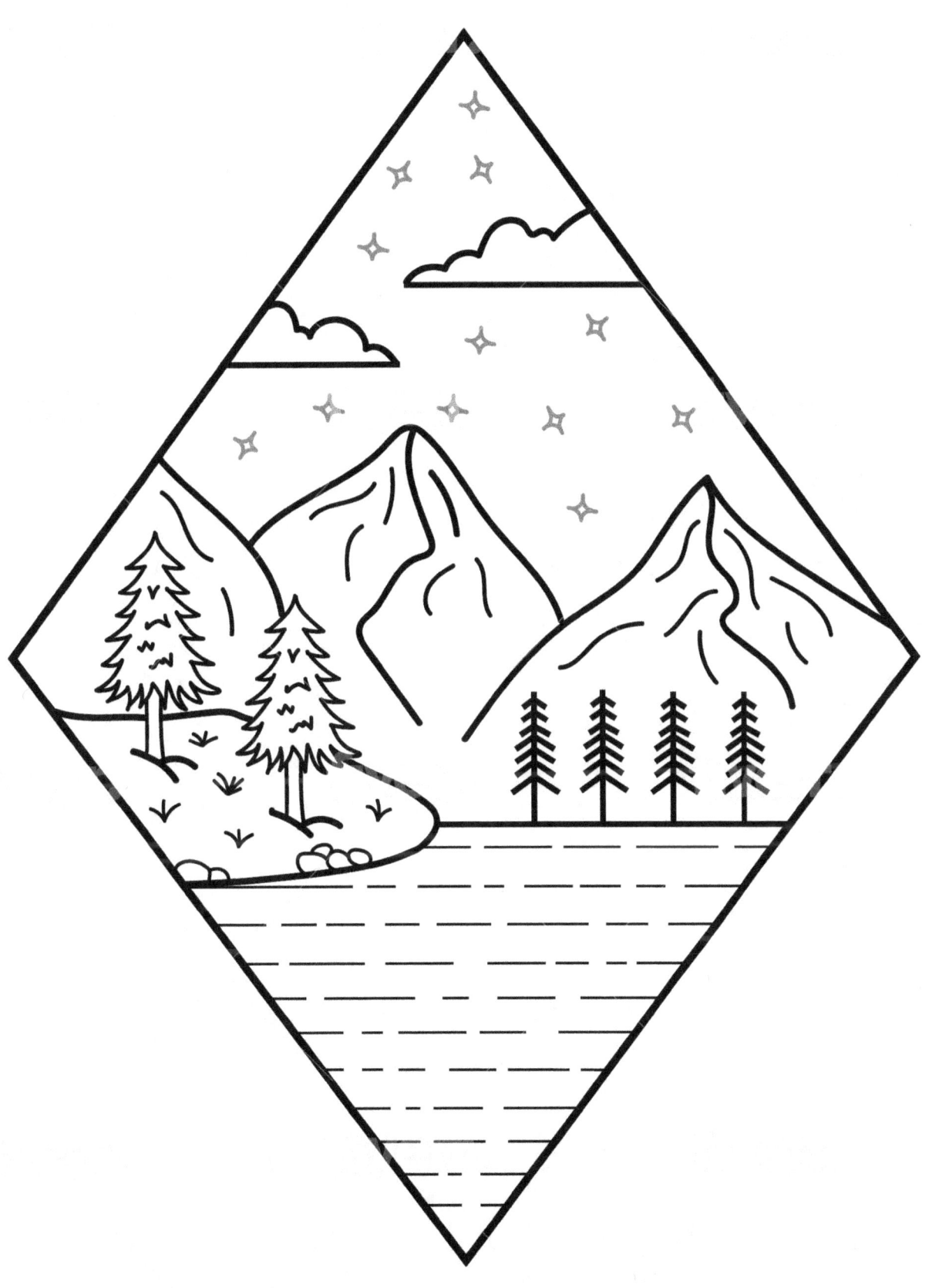

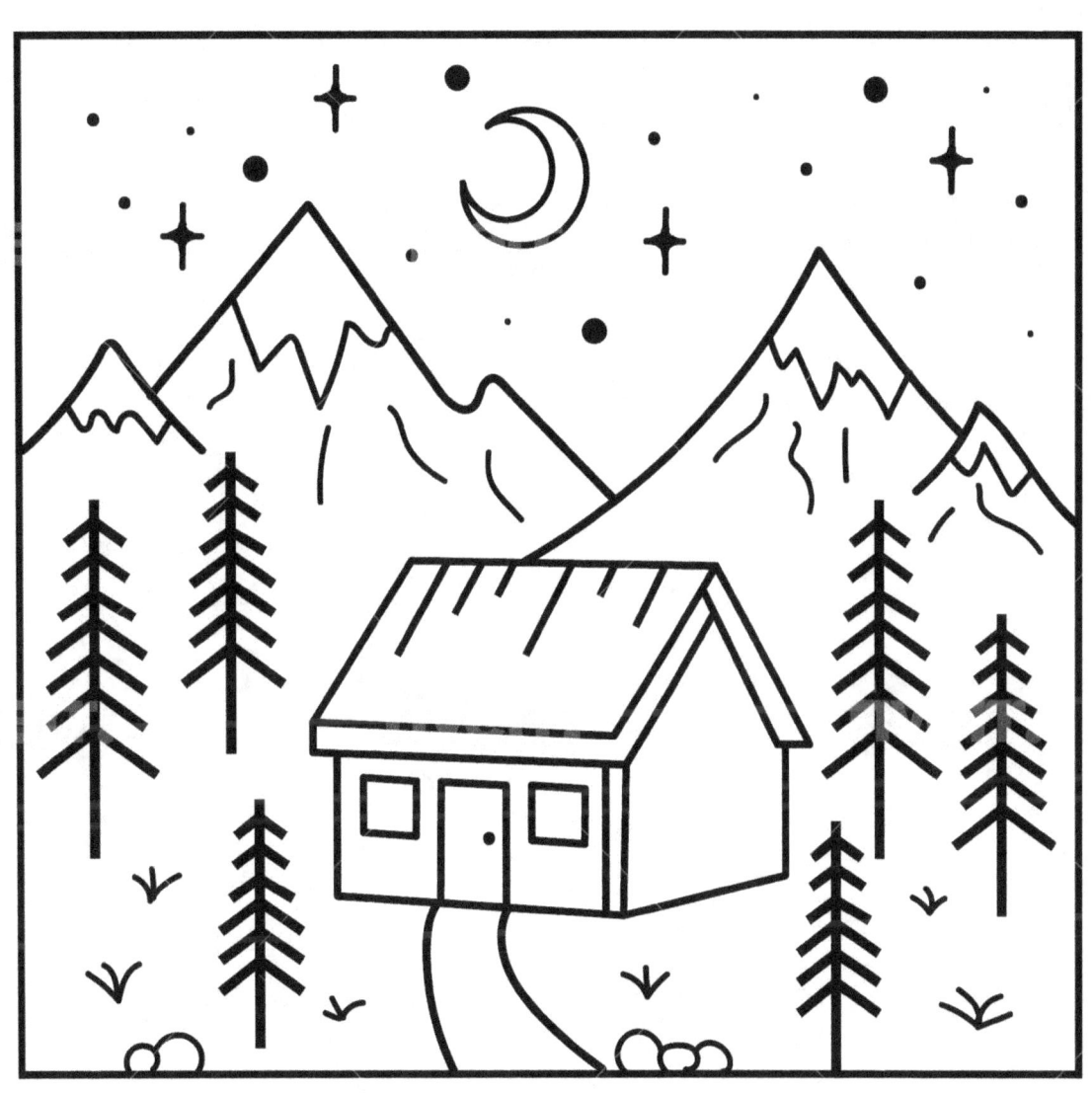

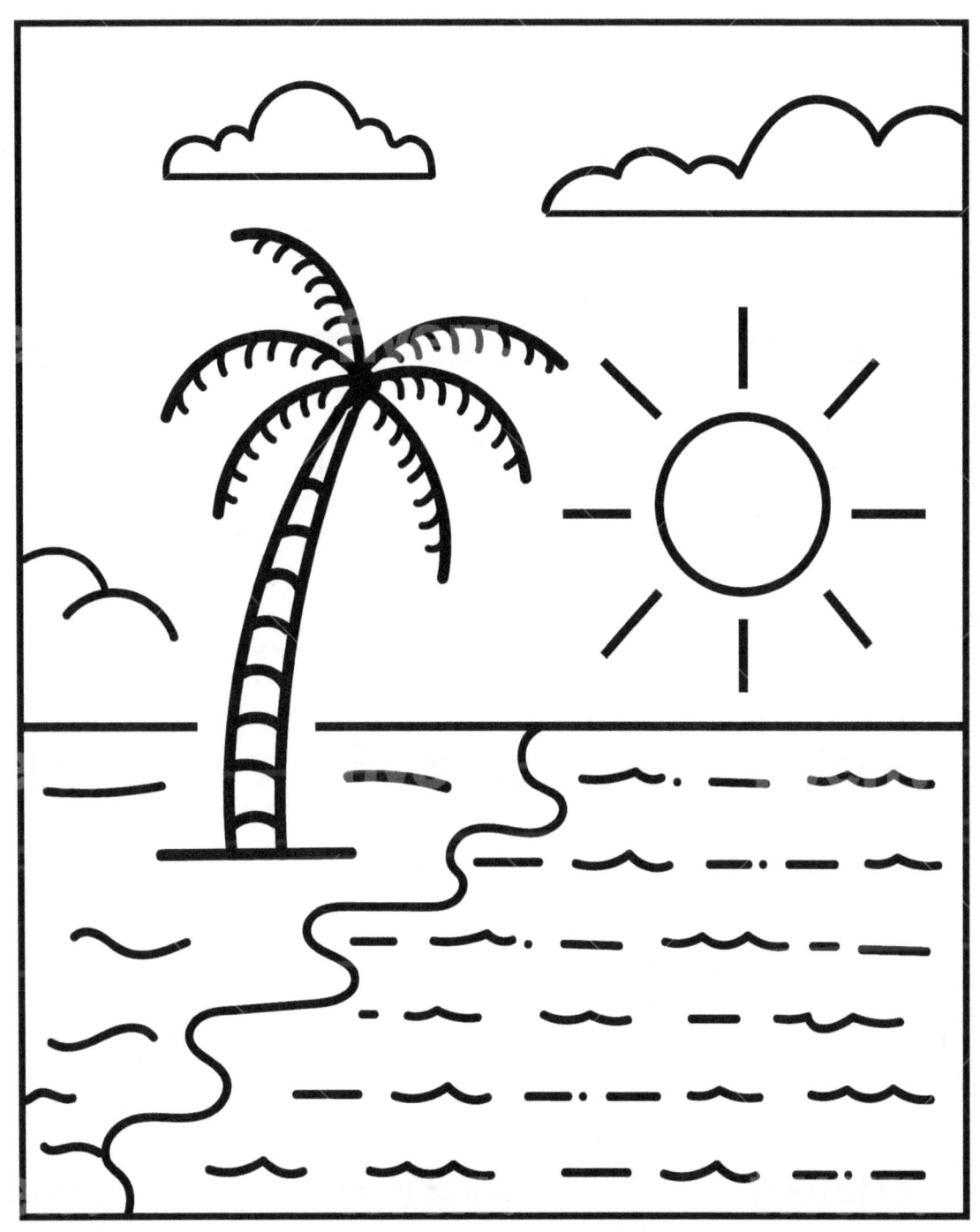

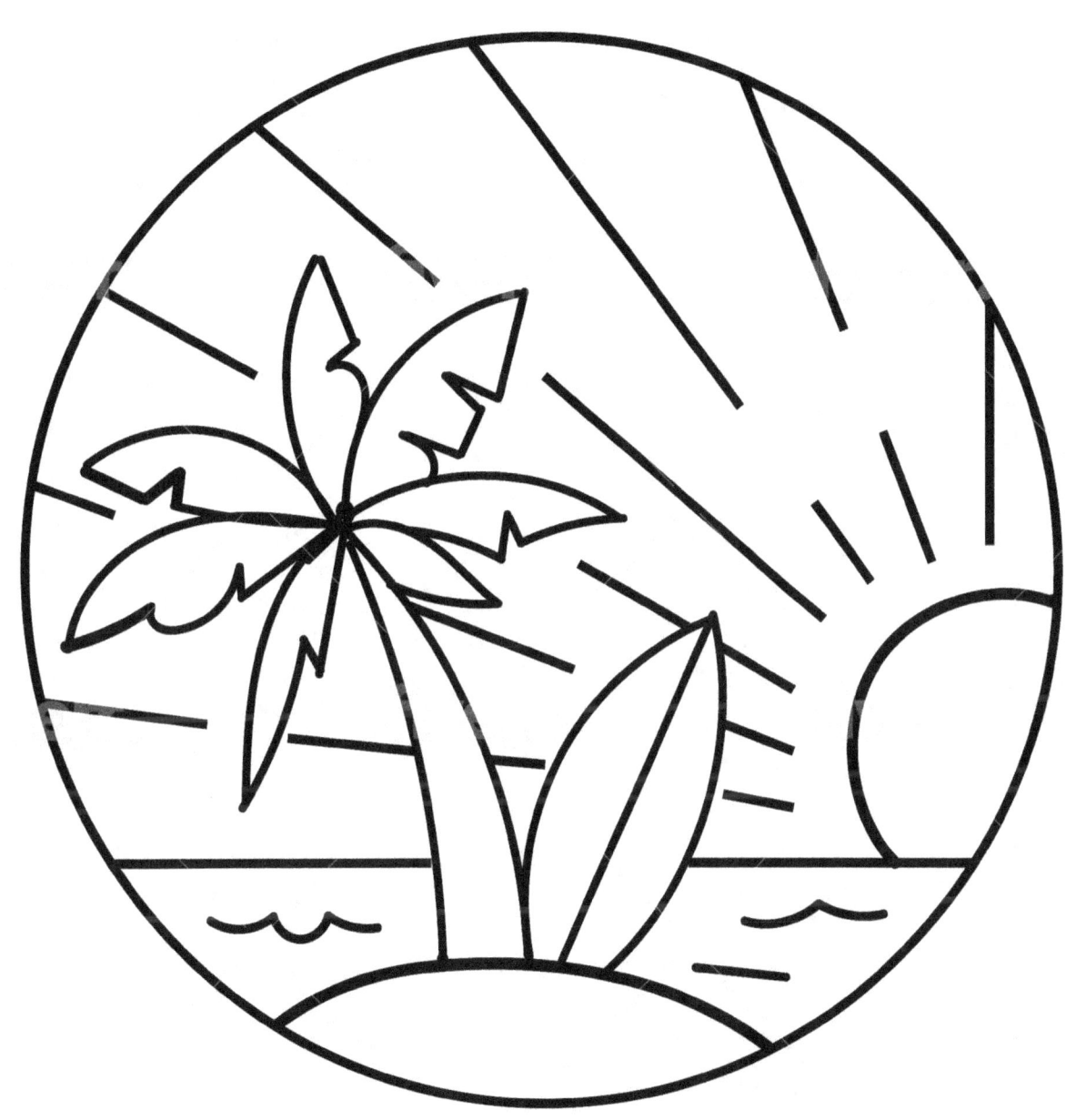

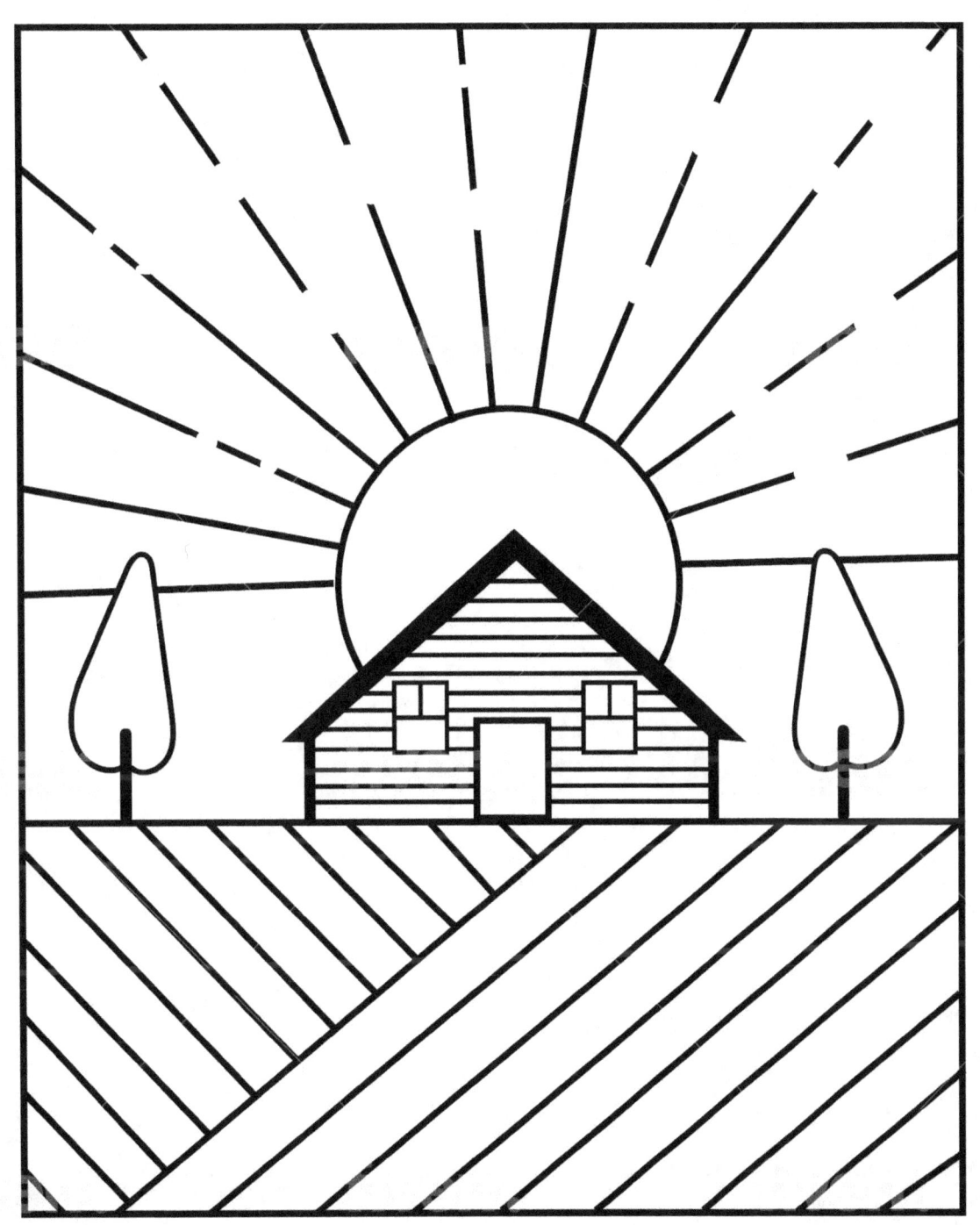

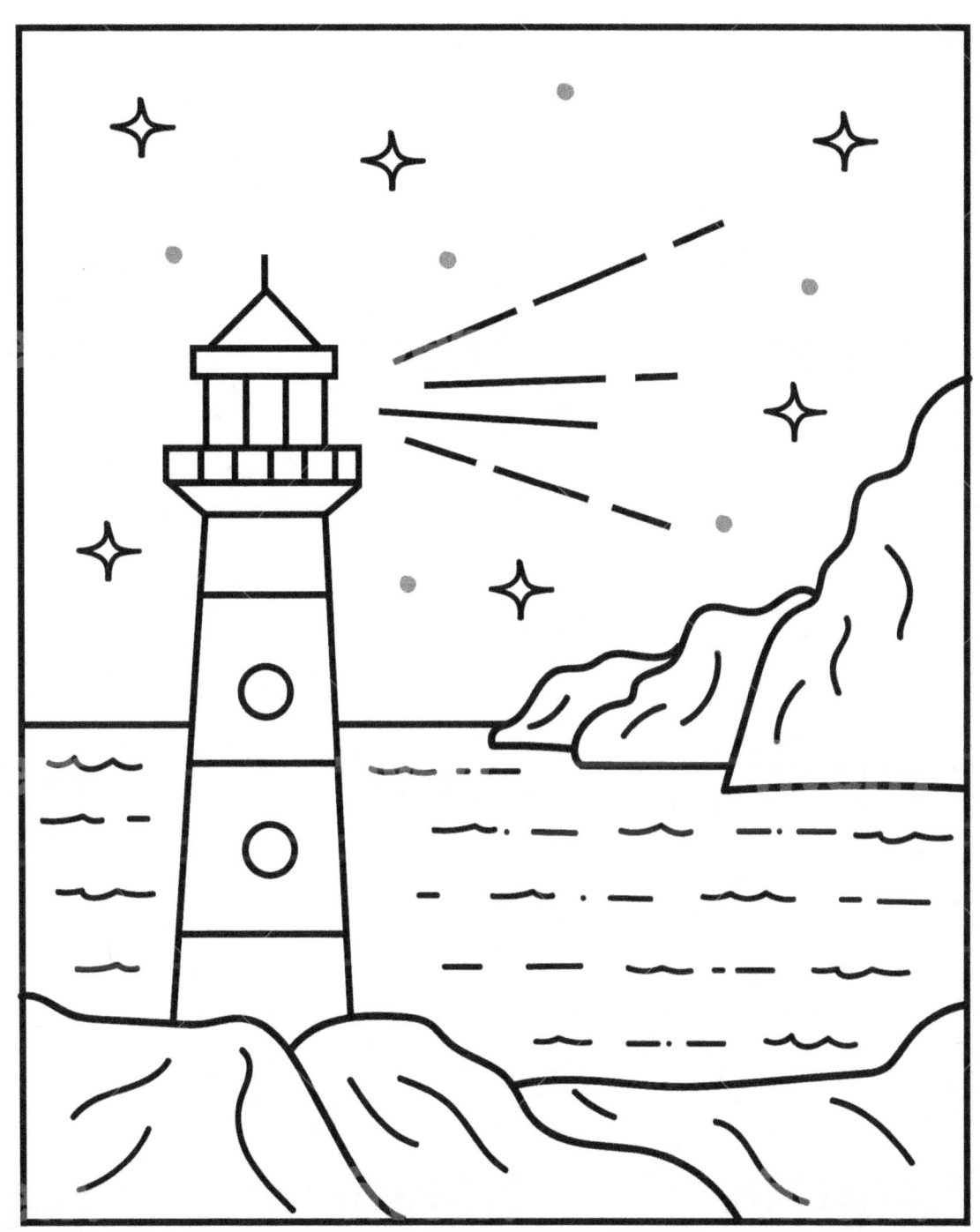

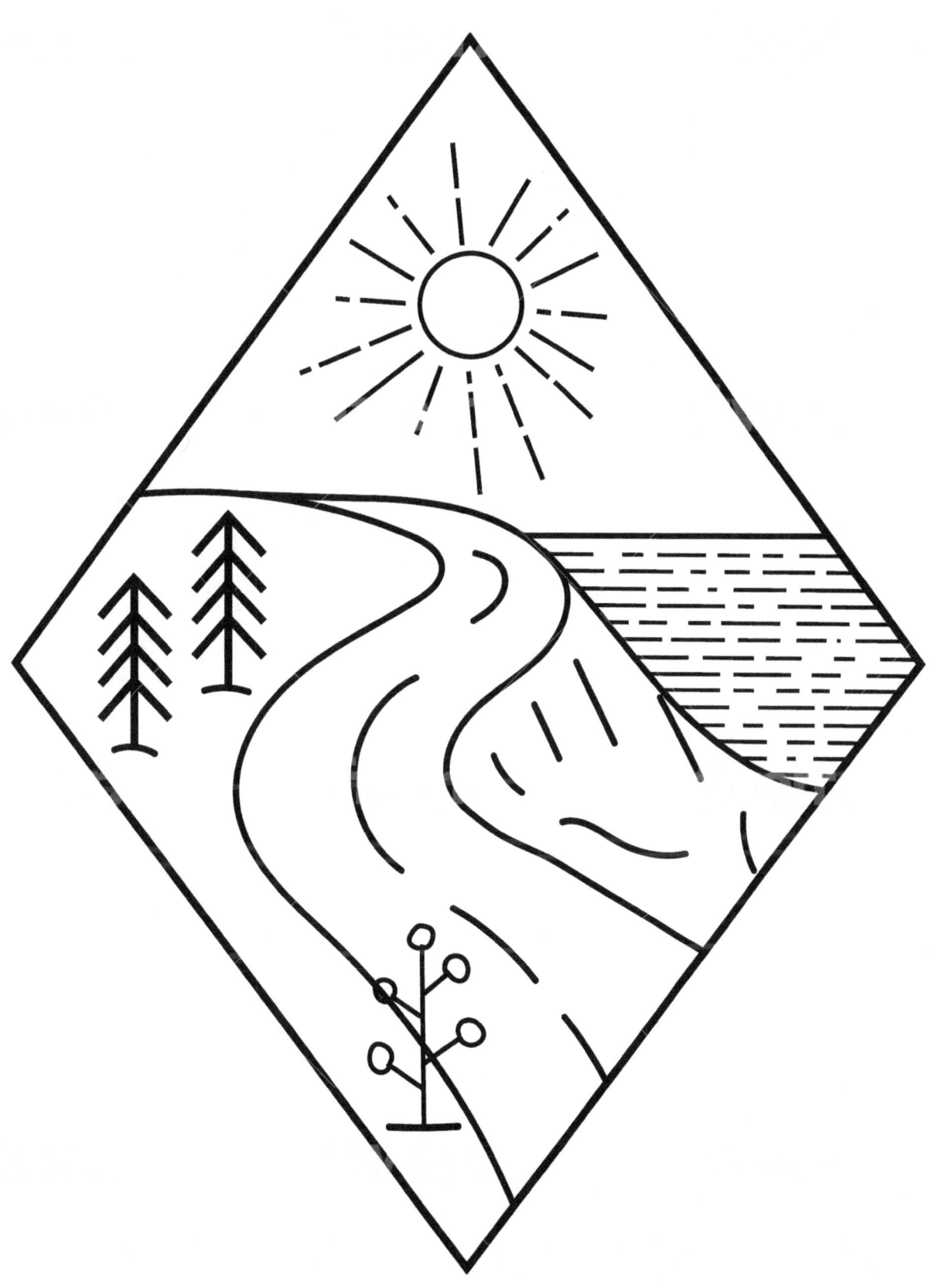

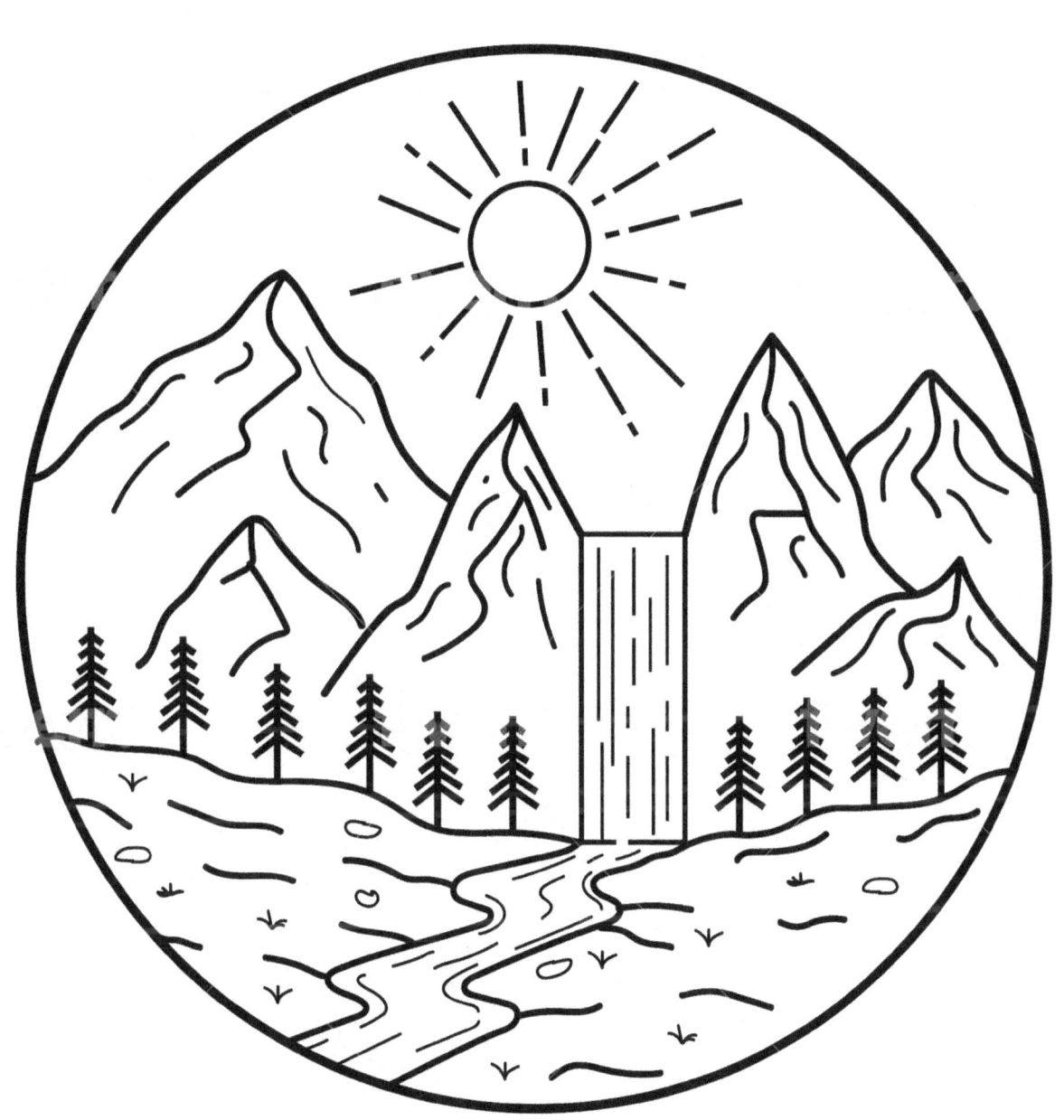

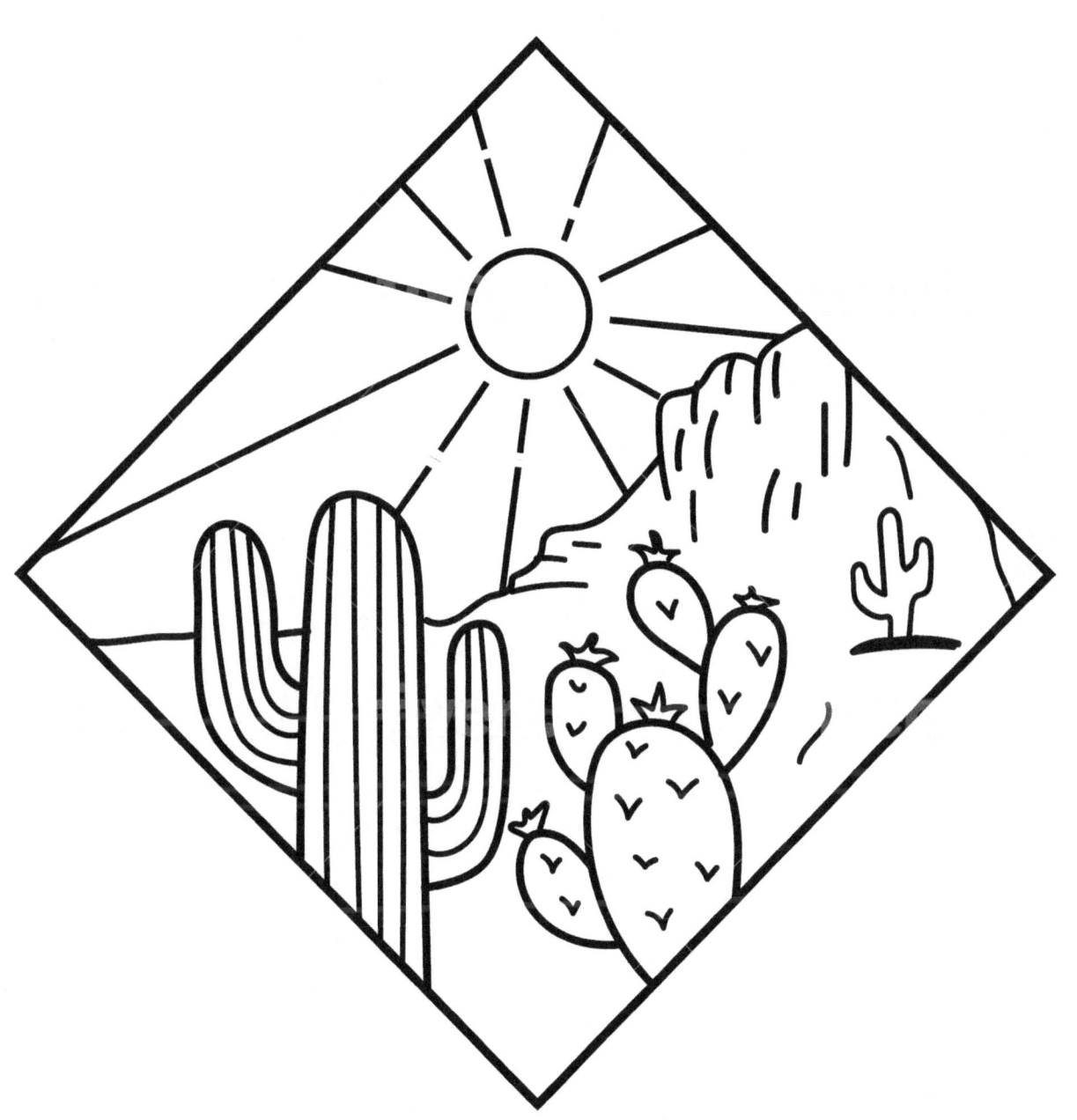

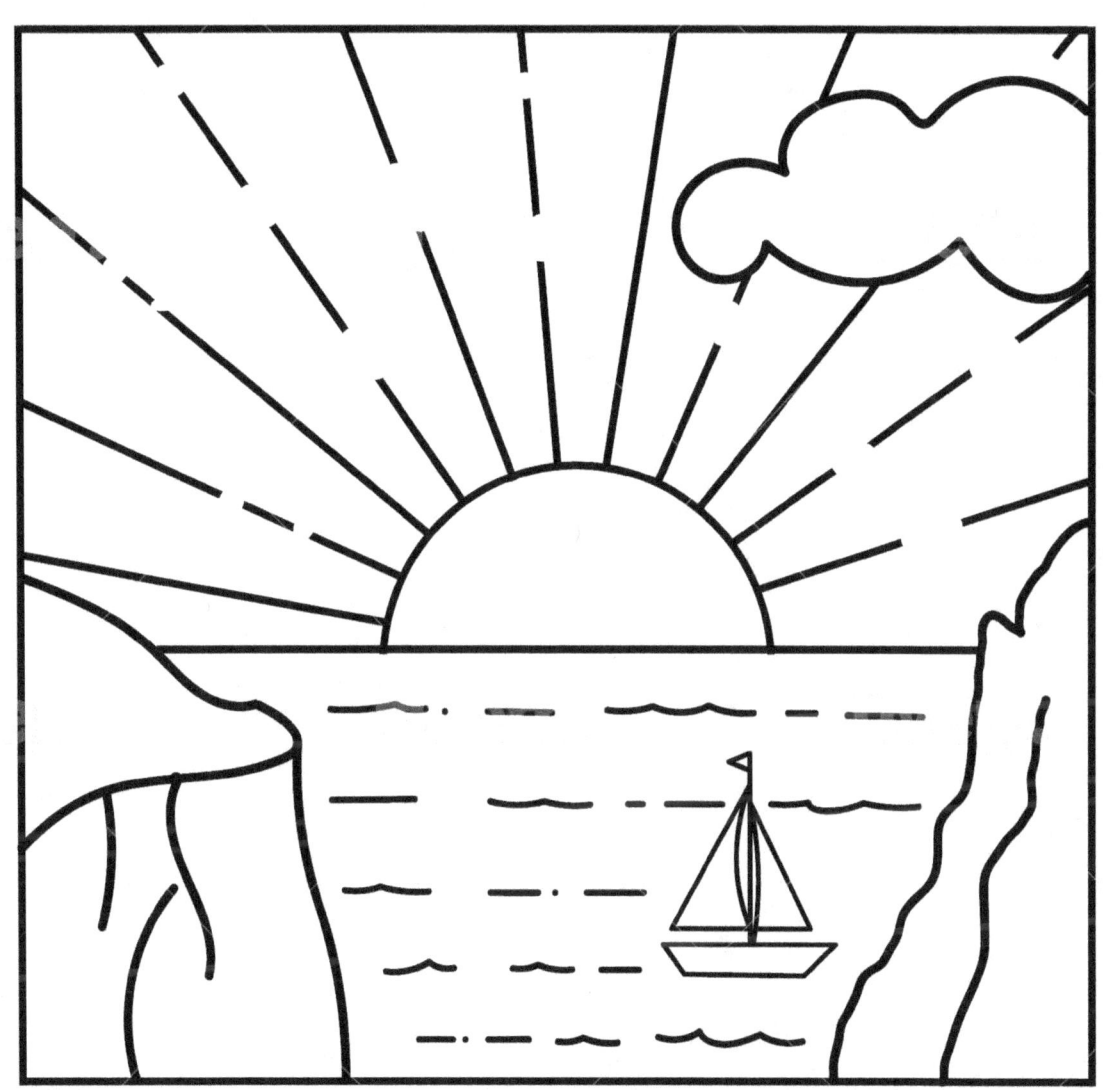

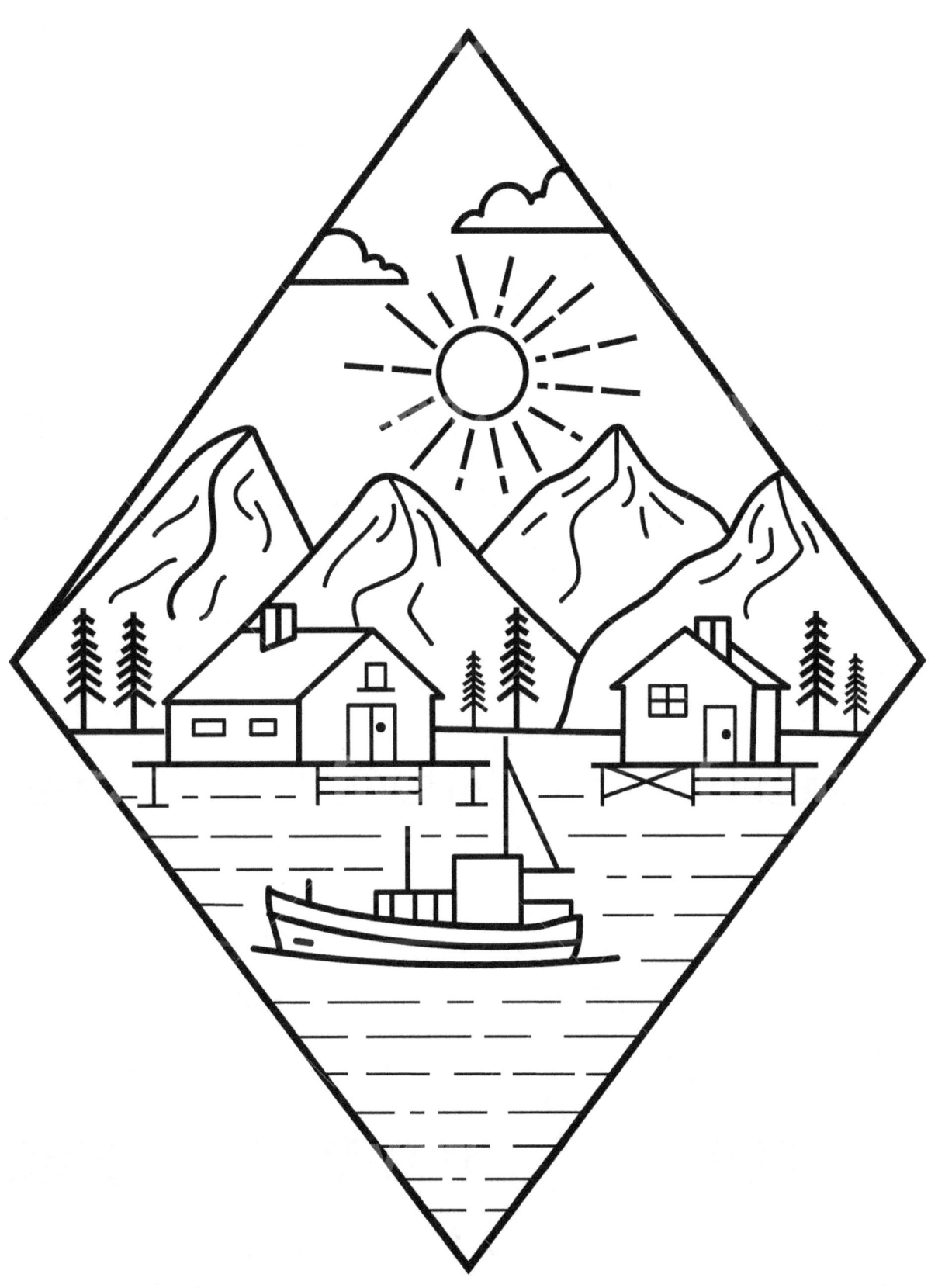

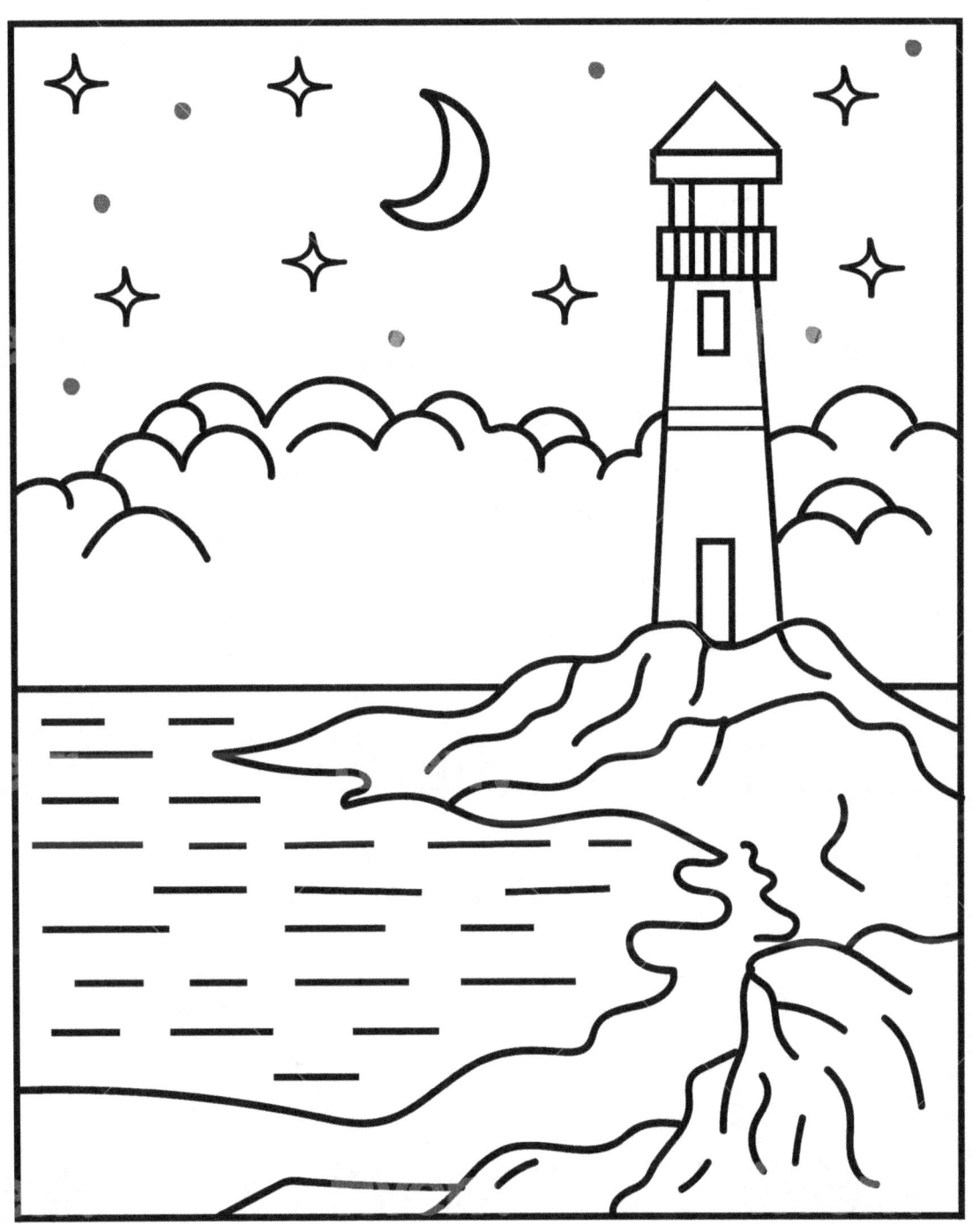

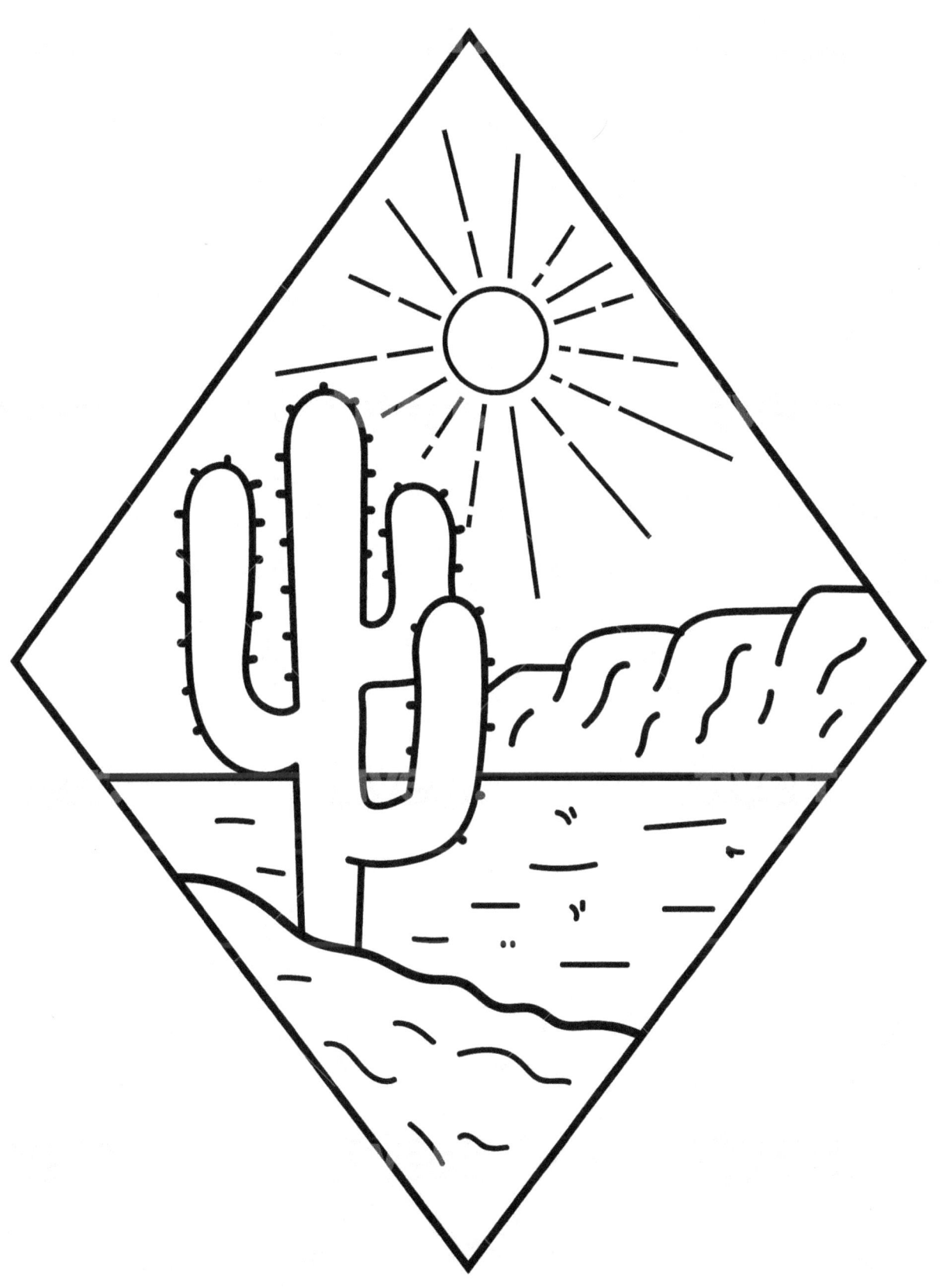

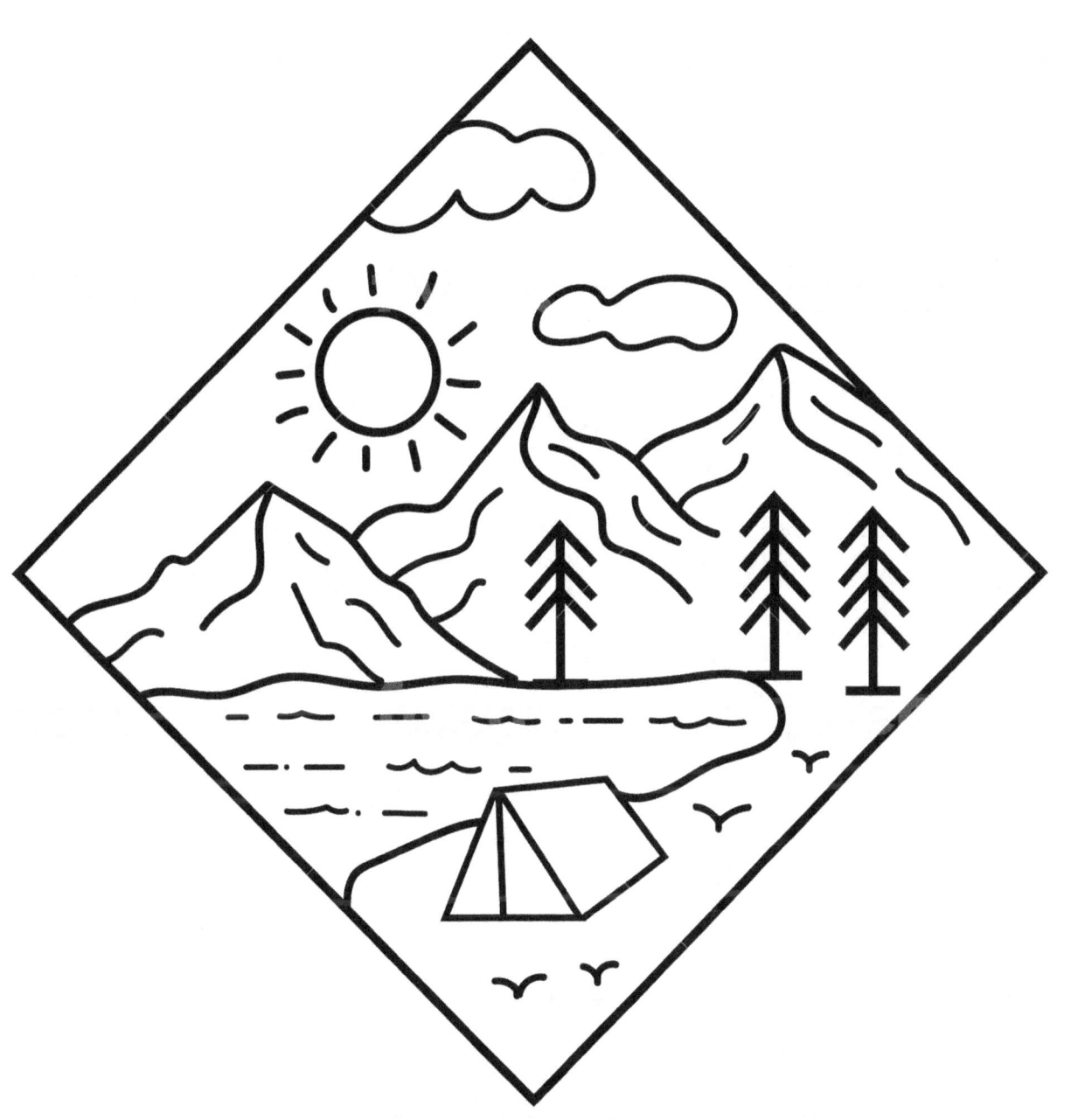

www.ingramcontent.com/pod-product-compliance
Lightning Source LLC
Chambersburg PA
CBHW082217220526
45470CB00010B/3212